Margins of GRACE

Becoming Champions of Faith and Family in the Midst of Disability

Margins of GRACE

Becoming Champions of Faith and Family in the Midst of Disability

Caregiver Edition

By Michelle Munger

Margins of Grace: Becoming Champions of Faith and Family in the Midst of Disability, Caregiver Edition © 2019 by Michelle Munger

Published by Candle's Flame Publishing 7 Victoria Sta, Newport News, VA 23608

Edited by Peter Lundell

Cover Art by Steven Munger

ISBN 978-1-7333970-0-1

To the moms and dads, family and friends
who are champions for someone in
the midst of disability.

Dear Reader,

So you got some news you were not expecting... In fact, you have been wondering when the doctor's office is going to call to say they had made a big mistake and were so sorry for the trouble they have caused. But they haven't called. In fact, you just got a referral authorization in the mail for a specialist.

They think they know why he isn't walking on his own, or talking. They think they know why he won't even try drinking milk, or won't sit still for more than two minutes. The labels are ominous and scary. The internet says life as you know it is over. As you snuggle with your little one, you cannot help but think of all the things he may not be able to do. I know I did. In that day there was no competing positive narrative. For me it caused a four year tail spin of simply trying to do the best I could for my children in the moment. I often look back and wish I had done so many things differently.

By reading this book, my goal is to provide encouragement and support. I know these words cannot take all the scary feelings away, but if you are ready, we will get through some of the toughest parts together. You don't have to do this alone!

You may not be able to see it right now, but it will get better. The world will be a better place because your child is in it. This I believe with all my heart. My experiences have shaped this optimism. My faith has molded my attitude. And faith is something that can sustain you through the adventure ahead. I am absolutely certain of it. I hope you will take my experiences and lessons learned and be an amazing champion for your loved one and your family.

With love,
Michelle

Table of Contents

Where I'm Coming From

When we decided I was supposed to write a book, I discovered memories of challenges can be depressing, especially when the worst seem to come from your faith family. I am sure I had packaged up all those depressing things and hid them in a deep dark basement. No one likes retrieving unhappy memories from dark places. The details I could remember were not something I wanted to unpack. I really did not want to shine a light on all the details enough to share them intelligently with others.

I had convinced myself I could handle life just the way it was. As much as I wanted to participate in a church, the reality of not being able to do so was somewhat paralyzing. We had gone without for so many years, and I did not see a chance for change. Even during my seminary education, most of my classmates had no frame of reference when I would bring up families like mine. In 2011 the awareness had not reached there yet. It seemed like an insurmountable obstacle that I wasn't convinced I could get around. When I pointed out how depressing the whole thing was, my husband sat contemplating for a moment. "Write. You only have to do it once." Gee, thanks dear!

But he was right. These stories and ideas should be shared. They need to be shared so others have an opportunity to see they are not alone. More importantly, I am now convinced we can change the world around us, one family, and one church at a time if we all understand a few truths. I wasn't prepared to advocate for my children and my family in church when they were little. I am now, and want you to be also.

I know you are likely exhausted and can't imagine doing one more thing. I hope you will find inspiration to push a little harder through the chaos. In looking back on my chaos, I wish I had done so many things differently. Circumstances can bury our perspective so deep, though, that we don't even realize we have a problem. I know I thought I was doing well at handling it all. But if I had done just a few things differently, early on, I am certain my challenges could have been more manageable.

When we have loved ones with challenges — whether spouse, children, parent or special friend — we learn to become "chef," "nurse," and "counselor." You will find as "champion" you will have an impact far greater than you can even imagine today.

My family stories will get us started. This book will explore ideas that will enable us to advocate better.

Then we will peek behind the ministry curtains so you will be able to influence your faith community in a positive and lasting way. We teach ourselves medical terms and research educational strategies to better advocate in the doctor's office or at school. Your church ministry leaders also have a language unique to their profession. Here you will find the necessary words to have a conversation about challenges and possible solutions. And finally, I provide suggestions of what you may need to help the church understand concerning this great big idea of fully including people with widely varying differences.

Our struggle is real but it is also very personal. Not only is it personal, our families are each unique. The accommodations we seek are not just for us though. When they are made available, everyone benefits. Together, we will approach this mission with confidence and grace—most importantly, with grace.

About the Author

I am passionate about many things, including faith, family, and crafting. My husband, Steven, and I were married in 1996 and have two children, both on the Autism Spectrum. Crafting is my creative escape with projects ranging from knit and crochet to glass enameling to silver wire working. I consider myself a confident disability advocate for my children's education and for inclusion within the Christian church. Steven is an amazing cheerleader who has nudged and pushed me toward sharing our experiences to help others navigate through the realities of living with or caring for someone with a disability.

The wonders of technology allowed me to complete a Bachelor's Degree in Family Studies from American Military University. Later you will see the motivation to pursue a Masters in Religious Education from Liberty Baptist Theological Seminary completed in 2013. Someday, I hope to return to the classroom in pursuit of a Doctoral degree from Gordon-Conwell.

We are a family of military heritage and strong faith. Those two children diagnosed with autism would shine a spotlight on the shortcomings of support in our society. The military way of moving every three years was not very compatible with the need for routine and consistency. Even in our faith communities, it was practically impossible to introduce the family to a new church with each move.

Navigating those realities, at least at the time of this writing, still requires extending lots of grace. The disability boundaries or margins need to be understood so we can then start to push and even adjust those expectations to match the freedoms everyone else takes for granted.

The Military Lifestyle Lens

Our story cannot be told without acknowledging the effects of being an active duty military family. This dynamic puts a spin on our experiences. While you may not be able to relate on all points, you may find parallels in your civilian lives. For us, we knew exactly what we were doing when Steven went off to the recruiter's office. Both of us were raised in military households and were very familiar with moving when the military said, to wherever they needed. I was not at all concerned about raising children while constantly moving.

As a member of the Active Duty Coast Guard, my husband served on two ships and three land based centers. The shipboard assignments meant they were deployed for one to three months at a time with short land breaks of two weeks to three months in between. The land-based centers meant he was usually home. The twelve-hour shifts that rotated between day and night, however, could be brutal when you have little ones that do not understand Daddy is trying to sleep and we should not play in that hall.

Military assignments usually do not take into account where family supports might be. The primary concern is where the skills of the member are needed. While family lived in Virginia, we were sent to California, New York, and Maine before coming home.

We bought a house and settled into the area, expecting to be able to move jobs without moving houses. We were certainly surprised to then get orders to Massachusetts! We had to make the tough decision to stay in our home in Virginia while Steven went off to fulfill his orders as a "geo-bachelor."

Every family deals with their unique challenges the best they know how. The military family usually has a few extras such as prolonged separations (sometimes with loved ones in harm's way), and expected relocations every two to four years. The military family has to be extra and overly prepared when advocating for their family member. The first time we moved after receiving a diagnosis, I had five months to prepare the next school division. We sent letters from every therapist, videos showing good, tough, and typical moments, and spent many hours on the phone, ensuring we were getting the best for our children with little to no lapse in care. I am certain our efforts to inform and prepare the new school district made a significant difference.

As you read our story remember:

◊ Family members were not available as helpers early on.

◊ Being deployed meant Daddy was away for long stretches of time, requiring me to behave much like a single mom.

If you are active duty military, be encouraged. You can do this!

Even if you are unable to relate to the nuances of a military lifestyle, you may find we share experiences if you are a single parent or simply deal with crazy work schedules. I am confident that we have gone through enough to be able to relate to just about anyone dealing with the challenges of a disability.

Sprinkled throughout this book are more in-depth details of things we have experienced. These stories are meant to give a heads-up to what may come and provide encouragement.

Every family deals
with their unique
challenges the best
they know how.

Chapter 1
Margins of Grace

Once upon a time there were no computers or word processing programs to help format writing assignments quickly and easily. We used a pen and notebook with wide or college ruled paper. The horizontal lines guided what we wrote. The vertical line showed us where to start each line and where to stop at the line that showed through the back side of the paper.

When we are young and just learning to write, many struggled to stay between those lines. Perhaps we forgot and crossed that line or didn't realize the word we started would go past the line. Some writing assignments may have received a lesser grade if those margins weren't taken seriously. For those who remember typewriters, we had to know when to stop typing and advance to the next line.

Just as in writing, we all operate within margins of some sort. We drive or ride in cars staying within the lines painted on a road. We walk (or should walk) within the painted crosswalk lines across a street. A one-inch margin is important for any paper that will be punched with holes and put in a binder. Otherwise the holes may cut out words needed for clarity.

Let's look at the www.dictionary.com definition of margins:

1. The space around the printed or written matter on a page.

2. An amount allowed or available beyond what is actually necessary.

3. A limit in condition, capacity, etc. beyond or below which something ceases to exist, be desirable, or be possible

4. A border or edge

Definitions two and three will be the focus for this conversation. Take a moment to consider the limits of acceptable behavior in places like theatres, the grocery store, or the worship hour at church.

Now a theatre's margins are obvious. You have to sit still, be quiet, don't play on your phone, or don't do anything that might disrupt the movie experience of others. If you are unable to do those things, you cannot stay.

Until you have children, you may not realize there are guidelines to follow in the grocery store. Disregard those rules and you will be punished by shaming eyes, heads shaking, or a mean word. Don't squeeze the bread, don't open the freezer doors unless you are ready to pick your item quickly, and especially don't allow a child to scream the whole time you are shopping.

For church, the guidelines may include sitting quietly in your seat or standing when appropriate, no dozing off during the message, and no crying or other distracting behaviors that would interfere with someone else's worship experience.

Many assume those unable to follow the rules, especially our children, are spoiled and undisciplined. But there is a growing percentage of our population who behave differently than desired because of natural, uncontrollable responses to their surroundings. The environment may be too loud, have too many flashing lights, or weird buzzing noises. Some brains may not be able to focus on a single voice when there are twelve different conversations happening in the room. Or even some may need to move around the room in order to hear and comprehend the story being read aloud instead of sitting quietly in a circle on the floor.

As a parent and advocate for my children and their challenges, I have discovered margins in life I never knew existed. I have also learned margins like those guidelines I list above are often so inflexible as to be completely exclusionary. We have left the theatre because it was too dark and too loud. We have endured the mean words while trying to shop for groceries with an extremely unhappy child. And we have been told we could not stay for Sunday school because the youngest would not listen to directions. These are the kinds of margins of life that, because of the attitudes of the enforcers, run contrary to families like mine being able to simply enjoy the world around us like most everyone else.

When an individual is unable to function within margins of expectations, they may be medically labeled as disabled. The language used today seems to change rapidly, courtesy of political correctness, personal preferences, or evolving terminology. We see terms like disabled, special needs, differently abled, and even the dreaded "r" word[1] used to refer to anyone with a challenge that may require an accommodation or extra patience from others.

We're going to look at some of the margins people with disabilities and their caregivers may experience. Every family situation and community is unique. We all need to know or check our margins. Once we know them, we may have to push on those margins a bit when it is obvious there are attitudes or other barriers preventing full participation in the community. And then the ultimate goal is adjusting the margins so everyone experiences life as equally as possible.

---

[1] The "r" word is "retarded," or "retard," and all its derogatory derivatives. It is so unpopular that it has been the object of many public campaigns asking the world to stop using the word to describe anything or anyone.

This is a journey into advocacy, into becoming a champion for another. It will be a process that will require lots of grace. Just as we looked at the definition of margins, we also need to have a clear understanding of grace.

Www.dictionary.com has many definitions of grace. Here are a few that pertain to this conversation:

1. Favor, or goodwill

2. Mercy, clemency, pardon

3. Favor shown in granting a delay or temporary immunity

And within the theological definition (also from www.dictionary.com) are:

a) A freely given, unmerited favor and love of God

b) The influence or spirit of God operating in humans to regenerate or strengthen them

c) The condition of being in God's favor or one of the elect

If we put these concepts of margins and grace together, I hope you will agree we have something to work with. We could explore forever what it would be to consider the amount of favor or goodwill allowed or available (grace) beyond what is actually necessary (margin). But then if we take into consideration theological definitions... is there such a thing as a cap or limit to the favor or goodwill we should extend to others?

Hmmm. Those may be tough concepts to chew on. As an advocate for my children and our family's life experiences, I have learned their disability is not the root cause of the problem. Society's attitude and response to their differences are huge contributors. This is primarily the tension between the medical models versus the social model of disability. The medical model says that a people are disabled by their impairments or differences. The social model says that disability is caused by the way society is organized.[2]

We must do what we can to change the narrative to declare every human being has value just as they are. I believe we can do that together if we honestly explore the margins we live in.

My experience of having two children diagnosed with a disability will provide a foundation for examining the challenges and evaluating solutions. We will:

---

2 "The Social Model Versus the Medical Model of Disability" www.disabilitynotthinghamshire.org.uk

Check our margins. Do we really know what we believe and how we will respond to those in our midst?

 Push our margins. What must happen to move us from where we are in our attitude and behavior about this topic to where we should be?

Adjust our margins. The big goal is to push hard enough toward lasting changes that show we value each and every human being through our actions of acceptance and inclusion. We will be proactive to include instead of reactive to an injustice.

We must do what
we can to change
the narrative to
declare every
human being has
value just as they
are.

Chapter 2
Understanding the Challenge

Michelle's Journey

I was expecting a normal life with normal children who would play normal sports. We would sell popcorn for the scout troop, go to wrestling matches in high school, or maybe wear earplugs while the band plays in the garage. Instead, my husband and I were blessed with not one but two boys on the Autism Spectrum. The older, Joshua was born in February of 1999. The younger, Matthias was two years after him. When they sat together as little ones, people thought they were twins. For the most part Joshua was quiet and mellow. Matthias, on the other hand, was a thrill seeker, always jumping, always pounding. His energy seemed never-ending. The children were both enrolled in public school early intervention programs. Therapy efforts were not enough to handle some of the toughest behaviors, and we finally turned to medication options. Medication was a tough route to choose. I did not want to be one of those parents who just drugged their kid to make my life easier. If we could help them conquer their challenges with therapy, we were going to do it. To this day, neither child expresses himself verbally. They do have a limited vocabulary and body language, but that doesn't get them very far with most people.

Shortly after Matthias was diagnosed, I attended a conference that promised to teach me everything I needed to know about this diagnosis and how to "cure" them. Upon sharing with one of the health food vendors at the conference that I had two children on the autism spectrum, they excitedly replied, "Boy, you hit the jackpot!"

Really?

So far the double diagnosis of autism made the simplest of things very hard. Both boys were incapable of carrying on a conversation. Shopping was a race to be done before the noises and lights completely overwhelmed them and they declared in their own boisterous way they wanted to go home. As a family of faith, I struggled with the realization our boys may never be able to understand who Jesus is and make a personal profession of faith. We couldn't attend church because none that we approached felt equipped to handle the boys' challenges. Additionally, my husband and I had not been out on a date night in years. We didn't know folks well enough nor trust enough to ask anyone to babysit. Moving around as an active duty military family simply did not allow us to make those kinds of connections. That vitamin peddler's quip about winning the jackpot did not ring true. I've heard stories about winning jackpots and I am pretty sure our experience was not even moderately close.

Alone in the Nursery

Joshua wasn't diagnosed until he was a little more than two years old. Our challenges began almost immediately though. The baby came home from the hospital. We said goodbye to visiting family who boarded the plane, very sad they couldn't stay longer. The tiny church we joined six months prior welcomed the little one with the love of a dozen grandmas. And then the music started. The baby started crying. Crying babies don't stay in the sanctuary of the church during a service. Immediately mom and baby exited out the side door.

This tiny mission church we fell in love with did have a nursery—a small building behind the church. As we spent more and more time out there, it became obvious this little building didn't start as a nursery. Its original life, we learned, was a tool shed. At some point within the previous ten years it had been converted to a sweet little nursery. It had just enough room for two rocking chairs, a crib, a small carpet, and toy box. The year was 1999, and I was glad that the space was wired to allow those in the nursery to hear what was happening in the sanctuary.

Unfortunately, though, there was a very strong musty odor, and the audio connection was nothing but static if it had rained within the last few days. And this was Northern California, where it rained a lot. And there I sat each Sunday, alone with my baby.

They say it's unhealthy to talk to oneself, but that's what happens when we're by ourselves. "It's okay. Steven is able to worship, and he'll tell me all about the message on the way home." This was true, except for the days when he wasn't home. He was an Active Duty Coast Guardsman stationed on a High Endurance Cutter. That meant he was deployed for two-to-three months at a time. There were times he was deployed for two months, home for two weeks, and then gone again for three months. So he wasn't able to relay the message often.

Typical Sunday conversations with myself would include things like, "Maybe today it will be okay." "Here we are again. Oh the audio is working today... actually it is not. Do I stay to say goodbye to people? Can I leave without going through the sanctuary? I think the gate is locked. Yeah, I'm trapped."

The weeks he was away were especially difficult. Each week I tried. But every single time, with the first musical notes, the first musical notes would elicit the most terrible wailing. I'd scoop up the baby, and out the door we went.

"Why am I getting up early, dressing my infant, and packing the diaper bag, only to sit in the nursery shed alone?"

With each passing Sunday I became more and more frustrated. Why didn't my kid like music? How can this be? His father and I had led the music at the chapel where we were married. We both loved to sing.

"You, little mister, are not allowed to not like music." And yet with each key played the cries got louder and more painful to hear. He must have been in pain. With music scattered throughout the entirety of the service, there really wasn't a good time to pop back in. The one-room-church building didn't even allow that option.

After quite a few months of this, I asked the question I never thought would escape my lips. My husband was deployed, and they had pulled into port that Sunday morning after a number of weeks at sea. He called about one o'clock when he knew I would be home. I was frustrated and now angry at having to sit in the nursery alone, again and again. I still can't believe I actually said these words: "I need you to give me permission not to go to church."[3]

---

[3] Yes, I did use those words. My husband is the spiritual head of our household, and I needed his guidance. This isn't usually how we begin these kinds of conversations, but it was a raw, emotional moment. See Colossians 3:18-19

You must understand just how alien those words were. I had been going to church forever. My first solo in the Christmas cantata with the adult choir was at the age of eight. That same year I had made my profession of faith. As a teenager, whenever the church doors were open, I was there. The first thing I did after settling into college was find the Christian campus ministry group. After I was married, my husband and I led the worship music together, taught Sunday school classes, led Vacation Bible School, and the list continues. We were involved.

When we arrived in California and found the tiny missional church, we knew that was the right place for us. I was pregnant, and everyone was so excited about welcoming a new baby. I jumped right in as the children's Sunday school teacher and even sang a few pieces of special music. My husband was given the opportunity to explore his calling of preaching.

But the baby was crying during the service. He couldn't stay; therefore, I couldn't stay.

"Why am I sitting there alone?" I said to my husband. "Why is the baby crying tears of pain every time the music starts? If I'm going to sit alone, I can do it at home in my pajamas. I'm done."

My husband listened quietly to my hysterics that had been building for many weeks while he was out of phone range. This wasn't the first time he was hearing about this. But it was the first time his wife had gotten hysterical about it. Through the tears I said, "I need you to give me permission not to go to church."

"Okay."

"Okay?" I almost couldn't wrap my head around the idea that my husband had just said it was okay for me to stop going. I cried. I cried both with relief I didn't have to endure the frustration anymore and yet also with incredible sadness that I wouldn't be going to church while he was deployed.

Taking Turns

Why we gravitated to small churches, I cannot tell you. We tried the big churches, and they just weren't for us. Usually they didn't have solutions for our challenges either, so they weren't any better. We arrived in New York City with a two-year-old and a six-month-old. New York would give us the official autism diagnosis for Joshua—and our new adventure officially began. We were very fortunate to live in military housing just down the hill from work and an on-base chapel. Like most military chapels it was small, cozy, warm, and loving. Not surprising, they didn't have the manpower to provide childcare, and children of all ages were sitting in the service.

I acknowledge I had strict ideas of what acceptable behavior looked like in a church setting. I am sure I knew that a two-year-old was quite incapable of doing any of those things, let alone an autistic two-year-old. Being cute and curious and even a little wiggly was normal. But we still had serious issues with noise levels. He simply couldn't stay in the same room with intermittent loud noises. My child couldn't conform to any of it, so all of us sitting together was not an option. But we needed to attend. Our solution? We took turns. After all, we only lived a couple of minutes down the hill. Depending on what was being discussed during the Sunday school hour, we would choose who got to go during which hour. We made the best of it by quite literally doing a high-five at the door of our apartment during the break. The most unexpected side effect of this arrangement was our discussion times. We discussed what we heard each Sunday morning much more because we were telling each other what the other had missed. Of course this is far from ideal, but it worked for us.

I often look back and wonder why we didn't do things differently. Why didn't we establish a support network and create the kinds of solutions necessary for us to attend church like normal people?

One reason was the tragedy of a terrorist attack so close to home. Just two short months after moving to the area, the Twin Towers in New York City were attacked on September 11, 2001. We lived close enough that we could see the smoke from our balcony and even hear the rumble when the towers collapsed. As much as we talked about not letting the terrorists win, they did stun the nation and our community for a long time. People were not gathering, were not volunteering, and were not doing much with neighbors. Everyone was staying close to home.

It was in the midst of this apathy that we found ourselves trying to cope. Our solution didn't require us to depend on anyone else. People knew what we were doing as we would often hear silly comments about Steven and me being the same person since we were hardly ever seen together. No one took any steps to help us, though. Besides, it was our problem to handle, wasn't it?

The chapel certainly could have done some things differently in its response to the tragedy of September 11 and our needs. And we can speculate all day long what we wish we had done. But, what truly matters is being on guard to use what we have learned to make a better future.

Exhausted and Alone

The first challenge was being alone in the nursery with my baby. The second big ordeal was attending a church that couldn't handle our specific family challenges. Taking turns attending got old, but it was the best we had. The next duty station sent us to the northeast region of the United States that boasted a small town feel and a tourist thoroughfare. There weren't many churches to choose from, and I quickly discovered that I didn't have the energy to do a lot of scouting this time around.

My husband was stationed on a ship again, which meant he was away for at least half of the year. I was essentially functioning like a single parent during those years. Both boys were enrolled in the most ideal special education program available. Preschool for Matthias was a thirty-minute ride each way. Somehow the schedules between the two boys meshed perfectly so I was able to handle it on my own when necessary.

The priority at that moment was healthy and happy children. We were now dealing with some pretty tough behaviors that made it quite impossible to leave them with anyone. It was so much easier to relax at home than try to function in public. The phone calls made to local churches proved it was going to take a whole lot of effort on my part to be part of a church but I didn't even know where to start. I just didn't have it in me.

I was exhausted. And half of the time I was alone.

Seven months before moving I said something about church in casual conversation and was told about a church near the school. One of the teachers attended there, and they were in the middle of planning and training to be able to welcome families like mine. They invited me to share a bit at the mandatory training they were doing for their workers a couple of weeks later. It was revolutionary for me. It should not have been but it was. For the last six months of our stay there, we traveled fifty minutes each way to church. We were finally welcome.

A Faith Home

After finishing my Master's Degree in Religious Education, I set out to find a church to serve as Children and Family Director or something along those lines. I was casting a super wide net, not at all worrying about which denomination I was applying to. If they were of protestant Christian beliefs, I sent a resume.

My first place of ministry after getting my degree was in the denomination of my youth. We mitigated the needs of my boys mostly by keeping them with me. We managed that for about a year and a half. It wasn't at all what the boys needed, but none of us knew how to do anything differently. I wasn't meant to stay there, though, and started the search again.

I sent a résumé off to a church whose denomination was only about thirty years old, and it was very close to everything for which my husband and I had been looking for years. When I wasn't called to serve in that church, we looked around to see if there were any of those churches in our area. And sure enough, there was!

This time, we didn't call ahead. We didn't ask anyone if it was okay. We just showed up like any new family would. Truly, I wasn't worried about calling ahead because the challenges that had kept us away were gone thanks to therapy efforts, medication, and maturity. As older teenagers, they were now able to sit with us just fine with the aid of technology and favorite books we brought from home.

For the first time in over fifteen years we were sitting together in worship. We were welcomed. We were loved. We had found a welcoming faith home.

Checking my Margins

I realize now that for some reason I felt the problem was mine alone to solve.

◊ Why should the church be required to bend to suit my needs?

◊ It's my kid causing the distraction. Therefore, he simply needs to be removed from the situation.

◊ The church is already stretched thin on people and money. No one else needed to use the nursery. "Is it fair to ask them to spend money on this? They didn't have to fix it just for me, did they?"

These were the questions and rationales I was using to explain and justify what was happening. I had a completely unhealthy understanding of my value to the church.

Checking your margins: What kinds of "rules" determine your involvement in certain scenarios? Do the rules change based on the company you keep?

 Pushing the Margins

Did you notice that at no point did I ask for help? I needed to communicate what was going on. No one can read minds. Expecting someone to do something when they have not been made aware is completely unfair. Unfortunately for me, no one else noticed the need to offer help either. If you have found yourself in a similar situation, here are some things you can do to help push these margins toward a better experience.

◊ Pray about the challenges.
　o Seek the Lord's guidance.
　o Seek an ally advocate to be made known to you that will help keep you included and feeling completely welcome.
◊ Calmly and with a graceful spirit make someone aware of the challenge.
◊ Help brainstorm low cost, easy solutions to get leadership thinking about doing things differently.

If I had had a healthier idea of what the church should do to support our needs, I may have tried a couple of things like:

◊ Find others worshiping at the chapel on Sunday morning willing to establish a small group time one evening a week. We really could have used an opportunity where we were experiencing and discussing life with other married couples. By meeting in a home, the kids could run about with few concerns.

◊ Be a part of creating family-friendly church activities. Sitting in the worship service for a small child is hardly ideal, especially if they have the "squirmies." Everyone would have benefited from a fun church activity that was kid friendly. Yes, that would have meant doing the work instead of simply participating, but we have to start somewhere.

So Here We Are

I hope you can see you are not alone. These may be bits of my story but they are not unique. Your challenges are shared by others. You do not have to do life alone.

Still, there is much work to do. We must push for a universal change in attitude about accommodating needs because it's the ethical and compassionate thing to do. Someone needs to start the conversation. If it does not come from someone on staff, guess what, it's up to us as parent or caregiver to advocate and champion the cause.

If you're ready, the next section will help you start thinking about the bigger picture in which you are a part. It is very much like those large portrait mosaics that are composed of tiny portraits. From afar you see one image. Up close, or even with a magnifying glass, you see all the unique images that together make the whole. The portrait of the church is incomplete if you are not connected to a body of believers. Let's fix that!

We must push for a
universal change in
attitude about
accommodating needs
because it's the ethical
and compassionate
thing to do.

Chapter 3
Work To Be Done

Getting Started

We are emotional beings. There is no getting around it. An unexpected diagnosis may immediately invoke fear. Unexpected and unhappy news conjures feelings we would rather never experience. Our response will determine our happiness or despair. And what we do with the challenge before us matters not only to us but also to everyone we contact.

As caregivers we have to guard against the crippling effects of our emotions. This is critical. Our ability to soldier on is needed by a few and expected by everyone else. If we do not hold it together, who will? We may feel overwhelmed by the need to hide or suppress our fears and feelings, but doing so is an unfortunate side effect of our current society's expectations.

Each of us will approach this challenge differently. People who don't fully understand a situation should not be telling others in that situation what to do. Yet there will always be those who offer or push their advice. So how do we handle it all? The first step is to take an inventory of our resources. These resources include our financial options and the people who care most about us.

Finances will dictate whether you wait for a conference to come to the local area or you hop on a plane. It will influence whether you buy that book or borrow it from the library. Our financial resources will also determine, unfortunately, options of medical interventions if those are needed.

Our people resources are our biggest, but sometimes most unpredictable, treasure. We often cannot know how another will respond to new realities. I was fortunate to have a loving husband with whom I could have a deep conversation. Yet we did not always see everything eye-to-eye as we were grasping at very different rates our new reality of two boys with autism. For all those early years I was the one attending meetings and doctor's appointments and making educational decisions. There was always a lot of explaining or catching up to do. Nurture your family ties, especially those who share your responsibilities. They and your dearest friends are a precious resource.

For some, an important people resource may be found within a support group. I acknowledge their power but emphasize it is not a one-size-fits-all solution. Find a group that is intentional about being positive and guards against heavy negativity. We all have struggles dealing with school administrators, counselors, and teachers. A support group can be an encouraging, helpful place to work through those challenges.

We must identify, guard, and protect our resources. It is so easy to burn through our financial assets in search of a "cure." If you go that route, be sure it is well spent on peer-reviewed, scientifically proven solutions on conditions that are actually curable.[4] And we don't want to burn out a friend or family member by asking too much of them in short amounts of time. Be sure the flow of conversation is open and honest. We'll explore more of this later.

A Progression of Attitude

As a mom who has been dealing with disability for so many years, I must assure you that my attitude and viewpoints have changed drastically over time. We go from panic and grief to acceptance and advocating; and the journey is not always pleasant. The main reason it is unpleasant is because the world around us seems to be against us. We fight for medical interventions. We fight for excellence in school. We fight to have a nice meal at

---

[4] Be very careful about jumping on the curable bandwagon. A diagnosis of autism, for example, is not a disease to be cured, but a reality to be embraced.

a restaurant with our family. And we even have to fight to attend a worship service.

Is it any wonder we are all in different places on a spectrum regarding our loved ones? Recently my husband, who is still curious about the cause, found a TED talk on autism. We watched it together. The speaker was a specialized pediatrician and she was discussing work on genome studies relating to the causation of autism. Essentially, she reported, no one knows what causes autism—yet.

Once upon a time, I wanted—no, needed—to know what had caused my babies to be different. At some point that wasn't so important anymore. I really just wanted them and those around them to be happy and able to co-exist. Lately I have found myself desiring the community to be more receptive and welcoming of my boys. Sure the boys need to learn certain skills, but the rest of us need to acknowledge that every human being has worth and deserves a spot at the table.[5]

My attitude changes were fostered by a few questions that begged for an answer. Why is it that those who are different are the only ones required to modify their behavior? Why do we have to force them to behave like everyone else? Why can't we celebrate, or

---

5 This table analogy is taken from one of my favorite chapters of Holy Scripture in the book of Luke. Chapter 14 is loaded with guiding information for how we should treat others unlike ourselves. Jesus' great banquet table parable is eventually seated with the outcasts of society, much like our loved ones with disabilities.

at least accept, our differences? After all, in the business world it is our differences that help us stand out from the crowd and gets us the job. Society's expectations seem quite fickle. You must be different but not too different.

I don't know who said it, but there is a wonderful quote out there that says, "It's okay to change your mind about anything when you have been given new information." As we grow and mature and learn from our experiences, our attitudes about many things can change.

Working through Grief

Have you heard of these "stages of grief?"

◊ Shock—numbness or initial response to unexpected news
◊ Denial/disbelief—difficulty believing what has happened
◊ Depression/sadness—acknowledging the sadness of the situation
◊ Bargaining—attempting to bargain for a preferred outcome
◊ Anger—response to questioning the fairness of the loss
◊ Yearning—desire for what was lost

It also seems our society needs labels for everything. With anything unexpected we may experience some level of shock and grief due to a perceived loss. The Mayo Clinic describes grief as both a universal and personal experience influenced by the nature of the loss.[6] An internet search on grief will initially give us information on five stages of grief made popular by the book *On Death and Dying*, by Kubler-Ross, published in 1969. Somehow this theory has maintained its popularity in spite of significant questions about its validity.

Fortunately, there have been subsequent studies done trying to understand grief and whether those five stages are real. One such study published in the *British Journal of Psychiatry* in 2008 suggests there are *states* of grief, not stages.[7] The experiences are not linear as Kubler-Ross suggested. Grief seems to manifest itself differently in us all. I suppose for some it is helpful to put a name on the feelings. It may also be especially helpful for our friends trying to help us as much as they can. An article on medical myths reassures us "there is no 'correct' or 'incorrect' way to grieve: the same experience isn't shared by everybody, nor should it be expected to."[8] The stages, again, are helpful to put a name on what we are experiencing, to give us

[6]https://www.mayoclinic.org/patient-visitor-guide/support-groups/what-is-grief

[7] The *British Journal of Psychiatry* (2008) 193, 435-437.

[8] "Are There Really Five Stages of Grief?" by Claudia Hammond. http://www.bbc.com/future/story/20130219-are-there-five-stages-of-grief

something to work through. A friend in the shock or even denial stage will need different supports than if they were in the depression or bargaining stage. Our goal is to be able to move forward in life without grief sabotaging everything we do. So how do we get there?

My personal journey did not feel much like grief when my boys were very young. I had anger mostly directed at doctors who tried to skirt around the issue. I tried bargaining and got a bit too close to pseudoscience, wondering if I had just done this thing differently or that thing differently, my babies would have been spared their fate. We spent hundreds of dollars attending conferences, trying to learn what had happened, and how to fix it. I also spent time in depression and a sense of loss for the future. No one could tell us what it would look like when they became teenagers or young adults. All we had to go on were the big challenges we had to deal with every day. The thought of having to work through those struggles for the rest of our lives was nothing short of exhausting.

That anger toward the medical community was finally addressed when I was invited to speak at an autism conference for military physicians and assistants as part of a four-parent panel. At the very end they gave each of us time to share a personal word. I can still see the auditorium and the faces of the other three parents. As I sat on the stage, I realized this would be a healing opportunity.

I began, "About eight years ago I received the diagnosis for my oldest son. Six months prior I was sitting with my husband, my two year old, and newborn in an office looking at preliminary interview test results with one of your colleagues. The medical officer said to me, 'I can assure you it isn't autism. You will want to get the full testing done soon though after you move.' That's all he said. I had never even heard of autism, but it was obvious we should be glad it wasn't that. At the bottom of the papers he gave us were written 'PDD-NOS' in big letters and even circled. While the internet was still young, it existed, and what do you think happened when I dialed up and typed in PDD-NOS? PDD-NOS is an acronym for Pervasive Developmental Delay—Not Otherwise Specified, and according to what I was reading, was the same as autism. Ladies and gentlemen, I was so angry that afternoon. I was angry because I felt lied to. I had so many more questions. Please, do not gloss over the truth of the inevitable, especially when it concerns our babies. Good, up-to-date information from reliable sources is needed quickly. Without it we delay valuable interventions and the support of our commands through the EFMP (Exceptional Family Member Program.) I am so glad autism is being taken seriously today. I trust you will all take what you have learned today back to your offices and be empowered to help families deal with their new realities."

After I was done, my heart was racing, my hands were shaking, and I had to take a few deliberate deep breaths. It was as if I had just won a knock out boxing match. Wow, did it feel good to share my experience.

Besides cathartic moments like those, I believe faith has a big role to play in overcoming our grief that may take root in many different ways. My faith finally reminded me that my boys were beloved creations in the sight of God. My boys are part of a plan and purpose of which I am privileged to be a part. Planned, chosen, loved—these are the words that tell me my boys are fine.

The world and our society dispute that idea. The pity, the misunderstandings, the snide comments—all speak brokenness and inferiority. And when we are tired, those things work as a pickaxe incessantly chipping away at that firm foundation of your faith. The world's *diagnosis* is not the problem. The world's (and even my, maybe our) *attitude* is the problem.

As much as we want to retreat to the safety of home and shield ourselves from the trauma inflicted by others, we must consider our need for connecting with people we genuinely love and respect. Our faith connections are especially important in this time. We need the support of a faith family to combat the awful ways our society tears us down.

Working through "Why Me"

Some of it is still overwhelming. As I mentioned earlier, I didn't realize I was signing up for this when we had children. My husband and I had long talks about how we were going to parent, discipline, not fight in front of anyone, have integrity with our decisions — all the things we're supposed to work out before they happen. Very quickly we learned that most of what we thought we were going to do wasn't applicable to our family.

I'm talking about things like the discipline we both grew up with that wasn't working. A key part of how discipline works is understanding cause and effect. Choices that result in a form of punishment should eventually decrease. We were dealing with no understanding of cause and effect, such as, "Eat the food in front of you or you'll go hungry." I had never seen the level of stubborn resolve before I witnessed my two-year-old refusing to eat scrambled eggs, or the five-year-old insisting on Cheetos for breakfast. Or maybe your kid will only eat Banquet chicken nuggets. (That one was interesting trying to figure out.) So yeah, the crazy things you are dealing with are "normal!" It's your family's normal.

We've had to figure out what life was going to look like for us. And everyone has an idea they think will work. Family and friends offer well-meaning suggestions that typically fall short because they do not understand the reality of our life. It is hard, very hard, to continually be polite with unsolicited advice. So many folks still don't understand that one of us, my husband or I, cannot hold a full-time job. We expect our boys will always need some level of supervision. Maybe someday that will change. In the meantime, the realities of our lifestyle dictate more than some people will ever understand. Every family experiences seasons of life. It may be sports season, band season, potty-training season, or whatever seems to be a central activity that impacts our lives. As with our weather seasons, eventually it changes.

When the diagnosis happens, the knee jerk response from most of us is "Why?" And a few months into the new struggle we begin to ask, "Why me?"

As you stand at the start of the Yellow Brick Road[9], there is only a vague idea of what to expect on the journey ahead. I have the great fortune to now be looking back on so many points of interest that a pattern has formed. It is a pattern that declared itself plainly as the handiwork of a loving creator. Each point of interest mattered. Every challenge or triumph played a part in who I am and who I am expected to be.

---

[9] The yellow brick road is a path in the movie *The Wizard of Oz* (1939) that Dorothy had to follow to reach the Wizard, the one who could help her solve her problem.

The great deceiver[10] would prefer we sit at home, angry at God for all our problems. We must resist those influences and embrace the idea that our loved ones are not broken in God's eyes and should not be in ours. They are made in the image of Christ. And there is a serious task for you to perform if you should accept.

This task requires us to understand a few things in scripture that will move us toward seeing God's grace and will for our lives.

In Psalm 121, the Psalmist tells us the Lord guards and watches over us as we go and come *for all time*. Can we stop for a moment and allow that promise to settle in our minds and hearts? We are not alone in anything we do! Not only are we not alone, we know that the Lord desires that we prosper, as found in Jeremiah 29:11, where it says, "For I know the plans I have for you, declares the Lord, plans for welfare and not for evil, to give you a future and a hope." Be careful though. This is not the same as society's definition of prosperity. This isn't about fancy cars and fat bank accounts. Scriptural prosperity results from following Jesus' commands to love God and love our neighbor as ourselves. These actions flow from faith and a way of thinking that embraces all of life. If we truly do those two things, how does that affect all the stuff and people in our lives? If we know that God loves us and takes

---

[10] See Revelation 12:9

care of us, we do not have to worry (Matthew 6). We can have joy in all circumstances (James 1), and the list goes on and on.

But we need to get serious about acknowledging there is a race set before each of us as Hebrews 12:1-3 says,

> *Therefore, since we are surrounded by so great a cloud of witnesses, let us also lay aside every weight, and sin which clings so closely, and let us run with endurance the race that is set before us, looking to Jesus, the founder and perfecter of our faith, who for the joy that was set before him endured the cross, despising the shame, and is seated at the right hand of the throne of God.*

Some get the 200-yard dash, some the 5K. Most of us get the marathon. My runner friends get super serious about training when they have made the commitment to run a marathon. They usually run six days a week. On long runs they carry weird snacks to help them push through exhaustion. Each practice run helps them gain the endurance necessary to finish the real event well. If we hold fast to the LORD as Scripture recommends, He will supply our endurance. We will recognize it as we grow in our relationship with our heavenly Father.

I can look back on my life thus far and see an amazing display of God's love. He has guided and directed. He has comforted and disciplined. He has inspired and equipped me for the work he has set before me.

Our challenges may be great, but our God is greater. I know my answer to the "why me" question. It stirs a sense of awe and excitement in my soul; awe in the incarnate God whom loves me and excitement over what is to come. Your journey to discover your answers to that question may take time. Each of us has been given a responsibility and the means to fulfill it all. But you won't do it alone. You will need your God. You will need your faith family.

Evaluating What Was Needed

I felt great excitement when I saw there was still a task with my name on it. But the excitement wore off quickly when I also discovered all the expertise I had collected thus far wouldn't be enough for the journey ahead.

While community experiences could be tough, most were navigated by sheer necessity. Just because a fellow shopper didn't appreciate my unhappy child screaming in the grocery store didn't mean I was going to leave before I was finished. I've seen enough eyes rolling to rival a Vegas slot machine. My biggest hurdle was church. I was a parent trying to get my family to worship. This should not have been so difficult. Phone calls yielded uneasy silence or meek voices explaining they weren't able to handle our challenges. They were confident the big church down the road would be able to help us. There were, of course, blatant problems with that suggestion.

First of all, we did not want to attend a big church down the road. We didn't like big churches before we had children and our challenges had not magically changed that fact. We had both grown up in small churches or the small military chapel. We valued truly knowing all the members enough to be concerned when they were absent more than two Sundays in a row. There is just something special and irreplaceable about the small worshiping community.

Second, there was an assumption that the big church had something in place to meet those needs. All too often, big churches are not any more equipped than small ones. Lots of people and big budgets do not equate quality Sunday experiences for a child or family dealing with significant challenges. One such big church we attended for about eight weeks used to call us on Thursday to see if we were going to be at church that Sunday. I understand the desire to be prepared. However, why wouldn't you just expect and prepare for us to be there? No other family in the church got called to check on their intended attendance unless they had a crucial job to perform, maybe. I couldn't even decide on what to have for dinner that evening, and the gal wanted me to let her know if my family would attend church three days in advance. Yes, they were trying. But for me, the phone calls reinforced the idea that my family was a burden instead of communicating we were welcome.

Third, why couldn't the small church handle our challenges? This was truly the million-dollar question for me. We cannot address what we do not fully understand. It was painfully obvious they did not understand the needs of people and their families with disabilities. It was also painful to realize that beyond our desire to attend worship, my husband and I did not know what we needed either.

Now you must remember this is all happening around the start of the twenty-first century. At the time of this writing, the disability community and our faith communities have grown. Attitudes are improving all the time. Unfortunately, it still seems to move at a snail's pace.

In order to prepare well for the task I thought I had in front of me, I decided to attend seminary. If I could not effect change as a parent, I would do so on staff somewhere. I signed myself up for the Master's in Religious Education at Liberty University. It only took me three years. I was motivated! Liberty is a great school, but I was surprised to discover that even between the years of 2010 and 2013, they were not talking about individuals or families dealing with disabilities. I can say that with great confidence because I think I took every children's ministry and discipleship class offered, and the subject was discussed only because I asked the question.[11]

After graduation, I set out to find that place where God intended for me to serve. I was searching for an education, children, or family ministry position in a church that wanted to be serious about including people with disabilities in their priorities. I sent countless résumés. I did finally land a part-time preschool and children's director position, but that wasn't meant to last. During the next search I had quite a few phone interviews that progressed to online chat interviews from places as far as Michigan, Arizona, and Texas. And then I got a serious interview invitation from a church in North Carolina. Close to the end of the face-to-face interview process, I was asked if I had ever thought about working in disability ministry specifically. My answer was, "Of course, but those spots are still practically non-existent. Even if there was a position out there, I expect I would need more experience before being considered." That interview ultimately did not end with a job, but it did introduce

---

[11] I asked the head of the children's ministry classes about this missing conversation and was told they were working on a module for one of the classes, so I expect it is better now.

my family to the denomination we would finally call home.

In our new church, the pastor and my husband decided I did not need to be connected to a single church. After considering all that I had experienced over the last few years, I had to agree with them. The expectation was now that perhaps I am supposed to be able to take my message on the road. How exciting would it be to be able to teach and be a consultant to churches on this subject? And then we got serious about the idea of writing a book.

Please do not hear me say I think you need to sign yourself up for a seminary education. It is absolutely clear to me now that a seminary degree is not necessary to make a difference. As we consider the particular race set before each of us, we need to know our obstacles and consider how we will overcome.

Decide What Is Most Important

No matter where you are in this journey as caregiver, you have to know what it is you need from others and be able to articulate sufficiently. The first "fail" experience I had was as a brand new mother in that nursery alone with my baby week in and week out.

It's amazing to me that as I remember that time in my life, *I completely failed to communicate I needed help.* I can't remember specifically asking someone to come sit with me. I didn't ask the sweet grandmother who usually sat on the third row if she would watch my baby once in a while. I never thought to suggest to the pastor that it was time to actively support a nursery rotation or even fix the audio static issue. I allowed myself to be completely miserable.

Because no one thought of a solution for me, and they couldn't read my mind, I just stopped going. Somehow I had convinced myself this was just the way it was. I did not have the right to burden others during the worship hour when it was obviously my problem to solve. In that moment, staying home and watching some famous preacher on TV sounded very inviting. To combat this trend, we must not be afraid to communicate our needs to the church and those who care about us. For a variety of reasons, the church may not always be accommodating or even quick to respond. But we must at least try before moving on.

Recently, when we were able to return to church as a family, I was asked, "How can we help you the most?" It had been so many years since my husband and I had been able to worship together that I didn't even know what to say besides, "Just allow us to worship as a family." That's what I really needed at that moment. I didn't need anyone to create a Sunday school class for the boys. They didn't have any kids their age anyway. I didn't need them occupied elsewhere during the service because they now could sit with us. We just needed to be accepted. The boys might make a few noises, they might stretch a little too long, and they might look at an electronic device quietly. "Would you let us join you without any frowny faces or head shaking or 'kidding' comments that we know aren't really kidding?" It was all we needed at that moment, and it worked to get us in the door and able to stay. Eventually the church added sensory tools like stress balls and mini plush animals the boys enjoy that the whole church was invited to use. And we have an additional print out of the words we sing for the boys to follow because they don't understand the screen has words we should be following. And as we go, we will continue to identify new ways to help the whole family worship together better.

Find Partners

Isn't it interesting how some of the best relationships seem to just happen? Whether at school, at the workplace, or even at church, we notice the people that seem to like the same things we do or volunteer for the same tasks, and they naturally become part of our lives. I like to think that friends are sent to us by God, who desires we be in relationship with others. Jesus sent the disciples out in groups of two. The buddy system was important to Jesus, and we need to understand its value in everyday things we struggle with on this journey with disability.

"Many hands make light work" is a common phrase, along with, "Two heads are better than one." Consider Ecclesiastes 4:9–12:

> *Two are better than one, because they have a good reward for their toil. For if they fall, one will lift up his fellow. But woe to him who is alone when he falls and has not another to lift him up! Again, if two lie together, they keep warm, but how can one keep warm alone? And though a man might prevail against one who is alone, two will withstand him – a threefold cord is not quickly broken.*

Friends are needed in this journey. Your lone voice in the forest of so many needs is easy to miss. If we give the benefit of the doubt, we can expect that no one is purposefully ignoring the need to include persons with disabilities in their activities. We also cannot ignore the fact that it may genuinely be hard for them to include us. How do we help people embrace those who may need a little more effort, especially when they already feel overwhelmed by what's expected of them? Isn't it interesting how we can always find room for that favorite food at Thanksgiving on a plate that's already heaping? The busiest among us have plates of responsibility that would rival a lavish Thanksgiving banquet, and we are certain we cannot add one more thing. Or perhaps we do one thing at a time. Our single rice bowl is all we can handle. Everything else must wait. When it comes to advocacy for ourselves and loved ones, this kind of discussion can't be considered a separate thing to make space for. It must be treated like the gravy to our mashed potatoes or the soy sauce for our rice. Otherwise, that entrée will never be as good without it. Stay tuned for more discussion about rice bowls in chapter five.

We need to find friends who understand the need. Those willing to roll up their sleeves and help will become obvious very quickly when you actually look for them. They will show a genuine interest in your family and hover close. Those people will be your allies. Remember to go slowly with them. They may be willing, but that doesn't mean they are ready to babysit for four hours the day after you meet. They will need information. You will need to arrange together time to see how everyone interacts and offer suggestions. Believe it or not, there are many things you do to communicate as a caregiver that you take for granted. Those small details are often the difference between a happy person and a meltdown. You might never think to add those things to a list for the care provider because you don't even realize you do them.

The things I am talking about, for example, might be body language or choices you make out of habit. Do you realize you may use the same sing-song tone and the exact same words each time you announce bed time? Have you thought about the fact that they get a snack two hours before bed and the youngest still requires you to use the red bowl? You know what will happen if you don't use the red bowl, but no one else does until it is too late; unless they have really had the chance to fully get to know the family.

It is very tough to expose your family on this level to others. When we have family members who also function as our support network, we do not seek out those kinds of partners in caring. *We do ourselves, and others who desire to be closest to us, a great disservice when we do not invite them into our world.* After all, if they aren't personally dealing with disabilities, how else will they learn what it really involves?

We must be willing to allow our brothers and sisters in Christ to come along side us in admittedly very personal ways. We must be willing to be vulnerable and humble. And we must trust that the partners God has chosen for the family will truly be a blessing. As long as everyone orients themselves toward God and His mercy and grace, everything will be fine.

> *I thank my God in all remembrance of you, always in every prayer of mine for you all making my prayer with joy, because of your partnership in the gospel from the first day until now. (Philippians 1:3–5).*

Checking the Margins

In this chapter, did anything jump out enough to circle or note it in your journal for extra thought later? Perhaps the grieving process has still got you caught in a loop. Or maybe, like me, you are still trying to figure out what is most important to you, so you will be able to communicate that when asked.

On the next page is a worksheet guide you may consider using. This exercise is all about checking our margins. What are the boundaries we have created for ourselves? A full size PDF version is available at www.marginsofgrace.com under resources.

Pushing the Margins

Now that we've had a bit of introspective time, consider tucking those answers in a safe place. Put a reminder somewhere, and in a year or two come back and look at the worksheet again. My hope is you will have managed to move forward and can identify how the margins that exist today have been pushed outward. You'll get the tools to do that in the upcoming chapters.

Chapter 3 Worksheet
My Personal Inventory

Finances:

People:

My attitude: I am _____ because of _____ and
        feel that _____ needs to change.

Am I grieving?

How would I answer these F.A.Q.'s?

How can they help me?

What do I need when _____?

How should they respond when _____?

Is there anything they should not do? _____

What makes _____smile?

What does _____ enjoy doing most?

Who are my allies?

Have I pushed someone away unintentionally?

Who do I need to show more grace?

We do ourselves,
and others who desire
to be closest to us, a
great disservice when
we do not invite them
into our world.

Chapter 4
Advocacy

Hindsight is amazingly clear. I look back and wish I had known more about myself. I wish someone had talked to me about what being a good advocate across all aspects of life would mean. And equally important, I wish someone who would have reminded me to take care of myself.

We need to be intentional advocates in four specific areas of life. Those areas are in the realms of education, family, faith, and self-care. Let's review the meaning of the word *advocate*. There are three noun definitions[12]. 1. A person who speaks or writes in support or defense of a person, cause, etc. 2. A person who pleads for or in behalf of another, intercessor, and 3. A person who pleads the cause of another in a court of law; and the verb definition: to speak or write in favor of, support or urge by argument, recommend publicly. Now keep these different definitions in mind as we go through this list of things of which we need to be intentional.

---

[12] www.dictionary.com

Advocate for Education

First, we need to educate ourselves. There was nothing more convincing to a doctor or teacher or therapist that I was interested and genuinely concerned about my child than showing them I was educating myself. That included reading, asking questions, attending conferences, asking more questions, and not being afraid to respectfully disagree.

Let me be clear that I did not assume to know more than the doctors about medical things.[13] What I did was ask questions. As an intelligent adult, if the answer did not make sense, we continued the conversation until it did. Often I would bring an article by the office and ask that we discuss it during the next visit. By doing so, I learned very quickly which doctors were consistently reading and learning about new things and which were not. I also learned who was unwilling to take the time to explain the why's behind certain things.

Just to give you a heads up, I am about to say something rather complimentary about Applied Behavior Analysis (ABA.) Now if you dislike or even hate ABA therapy for any reason, please don't toss this book into the fireplace just yet. I know and fully understand it is not for everyone. There are many self-

---

[13] I did have a moment of not believing doctors were telling the whole truth when I got too close to the pseudoscience lies, but that passed quickly.

advocating autistics who consider ABA therapy a form of torture! To add to the confusion, there are strategies people may think are ABA that are not. I personally believe in the need to identify the right strategy that works with a person's learning style. One size does not fit all.

But one of the best things I ever did was attend a conference on Applied Behavior Analysis. Applied Behavior Analysis is a system designed to support behavior modification. The therapists wanted to use certain ABA aspects to help my boys. By attending the conference, I learned the language and understood the pieces of the system and how it supposedly helped children with autism. That language and the concepts I learned have helped me contribute to almost every meeting I've ever had with a teacher or therapist.

You will discover that "knowing is half the battle," isn't just something 80's kids learned watching Saturday morning cartoons. An education, no matter the depth, is equipping. It will allow you to participate in conversations as a contributor and not just a spectator forced to go along with another's direction. Take science seriously. Be careful not to jump on bandwagons that can cause harm in the name of a promised cure. After all, is a cure really what is needed? What about empathy? What about grace?

Beware of Pseudoscience

Please be careful where you place your trust in the pursuit of education. Early in our diagnosis I was so intent on getting answers that I traveled to a conference on the opposite side of the country. At this conference I was told that the medical communities, insurance included, was only concerned about their bottom lines and were ultimately to blame for the epidemic of developmental delays rising in our country. They would say things about vaccine schedules and flu shots. And unfortunately, when I got home and tried to talk to the pediatrician, he could not answer any of my questions, inadvertently strengthening my suspicions.

At that conference they also tried to sell me vitamin packs and stool analysis kits and diet books that just so happened to be provided by the conference's sole sponsor. Imagine that. I fell for it, for a time. I fell for the idea that my children had a disease and needed to be cured. Autism used to be called a disease. And all those people at the conference made it sound as if I could cure them if I just did "this" or "that." It did not help that the medical community could not answer my questions. Everyone seemed to have theories. No one had many facts.

So whom do we believe? Even though the medical community was not doing needed research fast enough, friends of the "anti-vaxxers" and the specialized laboratories would occasionally say or promote something that just sounded wrong. Did they really believe that their treatment was worth the potentially life threatening side effects? Or, why were they okay with laying down the classic "bad parent" guilt trip if I did not spend $200 on a thirty-day supply of vitamins for both boys?

Eventually it comes down to common sense. If someone cannot prove that their experimental and highly dangerous treatment truly works for most, don't be the next test subject! We know that real science has done amazing things for humanity. Be sure what you are looking at is *real* science.

Educate Others

Every parent can be an advocate for their children. When challenges arise that separate our children from their peers, all the rules seem to change—and we must be involved. How do we know they are learning if they can't take the test everyone else does? How do we know they aren't being harassed or bullied when they can't tell us what's going on? When their challenges mean they are perceived as a threat to others, how do we prevent the behaviors that cause the fear before they even start?

I have a conference t-shirt that says, "I am my child's best advocate. What's your super power?"

Besides medical issues, the role as education advocate will be something that attempts to overwhelm and swallow us whole. We cannot ignore it or put it off for another day when public agencies are involved. It must be addressed every year. Every parent or caregiver wants the very best for their children. What should that look like in the context of school?

For many years the guiding principles have been summed up in two acronyms: F.A.P.E. and L.R.E. FAPE stands for Free Appropriate Public Education. Every child is supposed to have access to one. This right was granted by the Rehabilitation Act of 1973 and again in the Individuals with Disabilities Education Act in 1990. The key word we must focus on here is *appropriate*. The typical classroom setting may not be an appropriate placement, and therefore the school district must provide alternatives. Providing options is not something the district does out of the kindness of their heart. It is required by law. The second key word is *free*. The child's education, no matter the setting, must be free to the family.[14]

When trying to decide the best setting for a child's education, the other acronym becomes integral. LRE stands for Least Restrictive Environment. The LRE requirements have also been around since 1975 and included in the revised statutes of 1997 and 2004. Those

---

[14] Of course, free really means nothing additional. Within the United States, tax dollars support education.

guidelines want every child to receive their education as much as possible with non-disabled peers. The education team is required to think creatively if necessary to meet education needs in the most typical classroom setting possible.

Understanding FAPE and LRE will serve you well when it is I.E.P. time. Yep, it's another acronym. This one stands for Individualized Education Plan. Each child with a disability in the American public school system gets one. It details very specifically the educational goals and possible behavioral goals the student is working on. The IEP is also a federally recognized document accepted across state lines. An IEP developed in Maine must be followed in Virginia until it expires and the new team creates another.

For many the IEP meeting is a dreadful process. Stories abound of parents being ignored or school districts disregarding the law. I cannot personally describe that dreadfulness because I have never had a bad IEP meeting, even though I have had double the opportunity. I firmly believe that two things contributed to our good experiences. The first and most important was my faith. Personal prayer and a calm spirit of victory knowing we were going to do the best we could for my child set a tone for each meeting.

The second thing was understanding the law and knowing how to use that knowledge with grace. This was especially true for us as a military family. Every three years we were meeting with a new education team. I had to prove myself as a competent team player with each move. The first meeting was always in a suit or at least slacks and blouse. Picking up a small box of donuts on the way always helped ensure everyone was smiling at the start of the meeting.

I recommend an amazing resource out there that will help you be better prepared. Pick up the book, *From Emotions to Advocacy* by Peter and Pamela Wright.[15] I had the fortune of attending a two-day advocacy boot camp training the Wrights provided that was amazing for my confidence.

The first real IEP meeting I attended in a new state was also the first time I learned that good meetings were not normal. The school administrator actually said, "Wow. That was the best IEP meeting I've ever been in." Perhaps the letters from previous therapists and videos of good and bad moments helped them be better prepared. Perhaps it was my fervent prayers the night before and morning of. Perhaps it was all the reading and training I'd pursued. I expect it was all three.

Prior to each military relocation we were given almost four-to-six months' notice before the actual move. This allowed ample time to call the new school

---

[15] You can find the book and their training opportunities at www.wrightslaw.com

district and begin the process of planning for the next school year. Being prepared and proactive is an essential part of being a team player. *Never be afraid of giving them too much information.* It may also please you to know that eventually you can ditch the suit in favor of jeans and a nice shirt or blouse.

ABA Concepts & a Word of Caution

I mentioned ABA earlier and need to share one of the redeeming things from that system that has continued to give positive dividends. One of the breakthrough moments while learning about Applied Behavior Analysis was understanding the concept of "chaining." Chaining is where you break up a complex task into all the tiny steps that go into doing that task. If you are forward chaining, you begin teaching the task at the very first step. If you are backward chaining, you teach the last step first and work backward, doing all the steps leading up to that point for your student.

For example, have you ever thought about all the steps it takes to get a glass of milk? If you were trying to teach someone to get their own glass of milk, what do you think the first step is? What do you think the last step is? Many who try to answer this question say the first step is to get a glass. Well, how many steps are there in getting a glass? For those with a cognitive disability of any sort, seemingly simple tasks may be difficult to process and they may learn them best by breaking those tasks down into tiny steps.

The first basic step for many is traveling to the kitchen. For some students the actual first step is to process and understand they have to *stand up* and then *move*. After learning about chaining, I was able to give much better directions to my children, often times saying, "Stand up and come get your shoes on." Those concepts would prove invaluable when discussing goals with therapists. If I framed my concerns or suggestions using concepts like chaining, it was always received well.

One part of understanding ABA deserves a warning. When someone says they are using ABA therapy, they are talking about the overall system that helps them modify the behavior of others. Within the ABA system a variety of methods are used. The most popular in my experience is "Discreet Trial Training." This specific training requires the trainer to present a single task to the trainee usually up to ten times in succession. My favorite (and please hear my sarcasm) was "pick up the fork." There was a short period of time where I would hear those words echoing in the halls of my home they were said so much. I once told my husband he needed to be home during therapies because if I heard the therapist say, "Pick up the fork," one more time I was going to throw every fork we own in the garbage!

The goal is for the trainee to be able to respond to the request unassisted. When asked the first time, the trainer uses a hand-over-hand prompt to help the trainee do the thing. As time goes on, the prompts are supposed to decrease until they are no longer needed.

Joshua didn't mind discreet trial training. He was quick to understand what was expected of him. Matthias, however, did not care for it whatsoever. His behaviors weren't surprising. It was as if he was logically protesting his being asked to do this stupid thing that had no meaning beyond doing what the therapist asked over and over. Perhaps he was thinking, "I already did that the first time you asked, but okay, I'll do it again. What? Seriously, you want me to do it again? This is dumb." And he would throw the object in question.

Get to know the different methodologies of therapy out there to find which ones work best for your loved one. Again, one size does not fit all.

Incidentally, it should not have surprised us the first week we tried "Top Soccer," a kid's soccer experience for those with disabilities. There were college soccer players there to act as buddies. Matthias was sent over to do drills first. The first drill was to kick the ball into the net and go to the back of the line to do it again. We got to the front of the line and kicked the ball into the net with all smiles.

"Yay! You did it! Good job! Okay, come to the back of the line."

The smile faded when we got to the front of the line and had to kick it again. With a furrowed brow and an "uh, uh, uh!" he kicked it super hard and ran off to the parachute station, diving under it with glee.

Yeah, Matthias didn't like soccer drills. Or discreet trial training. I can't say I blame him. It also makes sense to see that autistic adults, who are able to communicate, also dislike discreet trials or any therapy models derived from Applied Behavior Analysis. One social media group I follow for autists and their allies specifically refers to any conversation involving ABA therapy as like that of hate speech and will not allow it on their site. They are very serious about the idea that a person's behavior does not need to be modified to "fit in."

Behaviors such as hand flapping, rocking in a chair, or humming are all targets of ABA therapy. They are also coping mechanisms, and no one should have to stop doing those things because it makes someone else uncomfortable. We would all do well to stop worrying so much about others or about what others think about us or about modifying someone's behavior to help them blend in.

Blending is boring.

Advocate for Family

Staying home is easy. It is comfortable. It is controlled. It is also unsustainable. You may feel staying home to avoid behaviors, both from your family member and from passers-by, is better than the alternative, but you must consider what you are sacrificing by doing so.

Going out exercises attitudes and enables strategy development. I had no choice but to take my two boys to the grocery store even though they hated it and let me and everyone else know it in their own way. With two little ones, I figured out I could put one in the seat and the other in the basket of the shopping cart, each with a blanket or stuffed animal—then behind me pull a second cart for the food. All that was missing was a train whistle. Most fellow shoppers thought it was great fun watching me maneuver this caravan. When the unhappy wailing started though, I had to ignore the side-eyes and disgusted looks as I kept moving and reminding my child we weren't done. I learned to shop at least four days after payday and to avoid Fridays, holidays or Super Bowl weekends.

Going to restaurants was extra special. We quickly learned that dinner was best at 4:30 p.m., before the crowd, and the kids' food needed to be ordered and brought out as soon as possible. Full tummies weren't so impatient. Even now, though we do not need to utilize these same strategies, we still often go at 4:30 p.m. because it's just a better experience all around.

When we venture out we not only exercise our own attitudes of what we are capable of accomplishing, we also help broaden the attitudes of others. Every successful outing becomes encouraging. Every person you are able to educate, no matter how they receive the information in that moment, may become an ally someday. Yes, there will be those who are ugly towards the family. We certainly do not irritate them intentionally, but their irritation is often a sign of selfishness, and that is something we can only, and must, ignore. People who express their annoyance directed at our differences need to be reminded they are not the center of the universe. The world does not revolve around them and their preferences. If everyone would simply mind their own business, the outings would be so much easier.

While it is not my responsibility to ensure anyone's happiness, we have to know where and when to draw the line on staying or leaving a situation. Grocery shopping, for me, was non-negotiable with my children. When my children were upset, I was certainly sorry they were unhappy, and subsequently making everyone around us unhappy, but my family had to eat, and I was not going to leave the store until I finished. Walking into a department store, though, with lights flickering and an intercom turned up way too high, became an immediate danger zone. I knew we weren't going to last ten minutes, so we just turned around immediately and went elsewhere. I once knew a young lady that absolutely could not handle sliding electronic doors. Understanding this, her mom found stores that did not have those doors. Eventually the young lady grew out of it, but for a season it was a tough ride.

Advocating for your family means you take a chance on going out and doing things—just like any other family. You only have to be more strategic. If your child never goes to a restaurant, he will never learn how to act in a restaurant. If they never go to the public jungle gym, they will never learn how to play on a public jungle gym.

Advocate for Faith

As a newly married couple we were sent off for training at a well-known Christian Retreat Center. The topic of the week was being bold in our faith. It was absolutely amazing. The whole experience changed us. I had always known I would someday work in full-time Christian ministry. After the conference my husband knew it too. That weekend, the little dream we had been given was to follow the model of Aquila and Priscilla[16] and lead a church someday together.

---

[16] You can read more about Priscilla and Aquila in Romans 16:3-4, Acts 18, 1 Corinthians 16:19, and 2 Timothy 4:19

When our first son, as a newborn, wouldn't sit through a service for any length of time, we started seeing a new set of challenges within the church. When he was subsequently diagnosed with autism, serious doubts about the future started creeping about. When the youngest was also diagnosed with autism associated with serious rage and impulse control issues, well, all our previous expectations crashed in a heap. There was no way we could be a family dealing with autism and also be leaders of a faith community. At the time, we felt they simply were not compatible.

It took the Lord about four years to break through the wall of preconceived expectations to tell me I still had a job to do. We couldn't go to church because of our disability. The disability affected us in many ways, from behaviors no one knew how to address to mommy simply being exhausted and unable to get out the door. What I needed from a church community did not seem to exist. How could that be? I couldn't be the only parent with disabled children with difficult behaviors. The number of children in the special preschool program proved I wasn't alone.

Where were they going to church?

They weren't.

I have learned we are incomplete without a faith family. Being part of a faith family used to be second nature to me. I could not remember a time in my childhood when we were not involved or looking to be involved in a church. That day I asked we not go anymore was the most bizarre day ever. How did my frustration level reach that point?

Hebrews 10:25 says we can't neglect to meet together or to encourage one another. And there are very important reasons for that command. Being disconnected from the body of Christ is first of all lonely. Having experienced that disconnect, I can say there was a definite void that could not be filled by other things. And it wasn't for lack of trying. I told a group of caregivers at a conference that if faith has ever been an important part of their lives before the challenges, it had to be a priority now.

Second, the community God places us within is intended to be a supportive, loving, and nurturing environment for *all* of us to grow. In today's technological world, it is far too easy to feel that we are staying connected when we really are not. Live worship and podcast recordings of the best bands, teachers, and preachers alive are available for free and within the comfort of our homes. I fully understand the allure. But let's look at that verse from Hebrews more closely.

And let us consider how to stir up one another to love and good works, not neglecting to meet together, as is the habit of some, but encouraging one another, and all

the more as you see the day drawing near.
(Hebrews 10:24, 25)

The command to not forsake the gathering of believers is about face-to-face encouraging and sharpening of one another. You cannot get that experience through a computer or television screen.

The flip side to this decision to stay home concerns the experience of the larger church body and how they respond to the family with a specific accommodation need. If you stay home, they don't have to worry about it. If you stay home, they won't have to make any changes. If you stay home, they will never have the opportunity to respond to others different from themselves. If you stay home, they may never understand what they are missing.

My children were not the first individuals with an autism diagnosis to attend and stay at our church. But they were the first with specific accommodation needs that were not previously provided. The congregation, especially those who continued to sit around us, learned to focus on the singing or the message rather than watching what the boys were doing. Sometimes the boys rock with the music; sometimes they look at pictures on their devices; often times they make noises. And while we as their parents try to temper their distractions, the others in attendance never expect the boys to be anything other than who they are.

Many Scriptures affirm the value and worth of every human being. I hope you will take a moment to pull out your Bible and look at all of 1 Corinthians 12 with me. We need to start at verse one. You should not skip this section about spiritual gifts. In verse six it says, "It is the same God who empowers them all in everyone." All have been given gifts. Not some. Not the abled. *All*. Hold onto that thought.

As you work down the chapter, Paul gets super serious about our faith connection needs in verse twelve. Please read this section slowly and even out loud. It is absolutely imperative we understand it fully. Verses fourteen to nineteen give this point from our perspective. "Because I am not an eye, I do not belong..." Verse twenty seems as if it could have concluded this section nicely, but Paul goes on. Verse twenty-one changes the focus. Now he addresses how we interact with others. "The eye cannot say to the hand, I have no need for you..." And verses twenty-two through twenty-five give us the big idea to this whole chapter.

> *On the contrary, the parts of the body that seem to be weaker are indispensable, and on those parts of the body that we think less honorable we bestow the greater honor, and our unpresentable parts are treated with greater modesty, which our more presentable parts do not require. But God has so*

composed the body, giving greater honor to the part that lacked it, that there may be no division in the body, but that the members may have the same care for one another. (1 Corinthians 12:22–25)

Our faith community needs us just as much as we need them. It is frustrating and disappointing when they do not understand. Have you considered you may be the advocate they need to, or will ever, hear from? It may feel like an impossible task, but remember, you are not alone. There is a God who is absolutely concerned for your family and families like yours. He is right there with you.

Advocate for Self

How do I take care of *me* today? Some days we will be able to say, "All I need is a cup of coffee, and I can tackle the day." Of course we may change our mind once the kids are up for an hour, but this section is about me time or self-care. It's a popular concept we did not used to hear much about, but it seems to have made its way into our culture. A quick internet search of the word *self-care* produces a variety of definitions, many links on how to improve it, and numerous articles claiming the millennial generation's obsession with it.[17] That obsession should not surprise us in the slightest. This new generation watched their parents and grandparents give and give and give until there was nothing left. Stay-at-home moms served their families with little to no regard of their own needs, which led to all sorts of mental and physical problems.[18] Those kids simply said, "I am important too. What about *me*?"

This concept needs to be something we consider consistently and honestly. Moms in general experience the same sorts of challenges and therefore have the same kinds of needs. But what about the mom dealing with disabilities that require therapists and paperwork and medical equipment? When you convince yourself you cannot take a vacation because your child can't miss the therapy sessions, then good, rational consideration of everyone's (read: your) needs isn't happening.

A self-care plan is an intentional conversation about how to be sure the caregiver is taking care of him/herself just as much as they are others. As with any advocacy task it may feel overwhelming. Each caregiver must have personal time. They must have a break from

---

[17] "The Millennial Obsession with Self-Care", 2017. https://www.npr.org/2017/06/04/531051473/the-millennial-obsession-with-self-care

[18] 2012 Gallup poll, "Stay-at-home moms report more depression, sadness, anger." https://news.gallop.com/poll/154685/stay-at-home-moms-report-depression-sadness-anger.aspx

their care duties in order to allow themselves to recharge mentally, physically, and spiritually. Often the attitude is, "We can't afford it," or, "We can't get away." Yet the answer should be, "We can't afford *not* to."

Personal time does not have to be alone time. Yes, some people completely recharge with a cup of tea and a book while sitting in the breeze on the balcony. Others enroll in a pottery class, surrounded by other artists who love to learn new things. Still others may log on to a weekly Bible study that meets online after the kids go to bed. This is really about identifying what recharges your batteries. When you know what that is, make it a priority, and do it often.

Don't wait until the body or mind decides it's had enough. We use the term "crash" for such situations. And do not wait for, or hope for, a convenient time. There will never be a convenient time. You must choose a time and simply get away, rest, recharge. No one else will, or can, do it for you.

When we are young and feel invincible, it is easy to ignore this issue. But the first time we break a bone or end up in the hospital usually serves as the wakeup call for our human limitations. Similarly, if we overextend ourselves as caregivers, we will, at some point, make ourselves unable to continue. Then who will do it? We absolutely must take care of ourselves.

I was on a women's retreat and found out one of the women had not been alone and away from her family in more than fifteen years! And she did not even have a family member with a disability. Her three children were widely scattered in age, so I understood the challenge. Still, I was in shock. I know if it had been me, I would have lost my sanity years earlier.

The first time my husband and I went on a trip without our children, Grandma and her husband came up to stay with the children for the eight days we planned to be away. Two days before we were scheduled to leave, the bickering started. My husband wasn't doing anything I felt necessary to prepare for our trip. Work was no excuse. The house was a mess. I didn't feel prepared, and departure time was coming, ready or not. The bickering continued even as we got into the van and drove away. Thirty minutes into the trip, my dear husband pulled off to the side of the interstate and demanded we address the attitude. My attitude. After poking at the problem a bit, we realized I was overwhelmed with anxiety over leaving my children. What if we die in a car wreck? What if they have to go to the hospital? What if…

You see, it had been seven years since we had done anything without a child in tow. Few date nights, no romantic lunches, no quiet walks on the beach. The active-duty military lifestyle is not always helpful for getting away when your family is hundreds of miles elsewhere. Tack on top of that the challenges of disability, and it was a perfect storm that kept us home.

Once we realized the root cause of my attitude, we were able to deal with those feelings through prayer and a regular schedule of checking in with home. We knew they would be fine. I needed to let go of my caregiver's sense of responsibility and enjoy the respite. As a couple we needed that time. A bonus was making time just for me. While husband was off doing things with buddies, I could do whatever I wanted. One afternoon, I chose to walk through shops and get an ice cream cone. I don't think I've ever enjoyed such a leisurely walk, and that was the best chocolate ice cream with strawberry sauce ever!

Find time for yourself. Find time to be with your significant other. Find time to recharge the relationships that recharge your batteries.

Creating a Self-Care Plan

Before we move from this self-care idea, let's do a little exercise together. You will need a pad of paper and pen.

1. Start with making a list of things that give you joy.
2. Now list those things that give you joy when you are alone.

◊ You may have to dig deep in the memory files for this one.

◊ This could be as simple as sitting on the porch on a breezy day with wind chimes and a favorite drink, or just taking a nap.

3. List your known and potential helpers along with the amount of time they are/may be available to help.

4. Get serious about monitoring how your days move along. What does today look like?

◊ How much time is spent scrolling through social media?

◊ TV time?

◊ Direct care of your loved one?

◊ Household chores?

◊ Travel time/errands away from the house?

This kind of inventory is essential for finding time for oneself that makes a positive impact on our well-being!

Now that you might be thoroughly depressed because it looks like you simply cannot fit one more thing into this mess, let's apply a bit of analysis to the things gobbling time.

◊ Can errand times be combined to a single day? Or even better, let someone else do them?

◊ Can chores be shared with, or delegated to, another household member on certain days?

◊ What if I used a timer to limit social media time in favor of another preferred activity?

◊ Is that TV show still great, or do I watch out of habit?

◊ Is there a tool or some other contraption out there that would make a task easier or less stressful?

Food prep time became so much more enjoyable when we bought new tools that worked efficiently. How simple. Large amounts of time were freed when we scheduled errands on a single day, allowing me to do creative things on other days. Cleaning was more tolerable when I started using a timer to break up the monotony. I learned a few neat tricks from a resource called Fly Lady (Finally Loving Yourself.) If you haven't yet heard of Fly Lady you must check it out. (www.flylady.net) Be intentional about paying attention to your time and spend it wisely.

Knowing what recharges our batteries is imperative for our well-being. Doing these things will have an immediate positive impact. When we are healthy, we will be better able to care for others.

Paperwork Rage

I must confess a personal consequence of not considering the full extent of unchecked stress and lack of self-care. There is this thing called paperwork.

Paperwork is unavoidable. Everywhere we go we have something that needs to be filled out. Usually it is basic contact information required for good record keeping. There seems to be a direct correlation between the amount of paperwork and current laws and regulations by which organizations must abide. More regulations equal more paperwork. I do understand why. The only way to prove you've done your part is to produce black-and-white written evidence reinforcing claims. But here's the thing: We are now living in the twenty-first century, and I am still filling out paperwork. We have digital platforms that remember every bit of information we type, even by accident. Why do I still need to use that paper and pen?

Sometimes I feel like going into a rage like that of a certain comic hero. With enough pokes or hurts, the mild mannered doctor erupts into green skin and muscles. My rage comes when I'm asked to use a blue or black ink pen to fill out a piece of paper giving the same information I gave last year, and the year before that. The information hasn't changed! Why can't they send me a link that lets me update the information directly? Why do they kill more trees to make paper that ends up being shredded after the information is entered into a computer? And why do they print out copies of yearly Individual Education Plans? Save it as a PDF and email it!

Ahem. Excuse me. Deep breaths... Okay, I am okay. See? Even talking about it makes me crazy.

I understand record keeping is important. We must know what is happening and how progress is being made. But I have notebooks and boxes full! I was never as excited at the end of an IEP meeting as when I learned I could finally get it digitally.

In the in-between moments of calm, that paperwork rage issue seems silly and frivolous. And I work very hard to suppress it. Now my husband is responsible for paperwork. Perhaps in time my inclination toward paperwork rage will disappear. I certainly hope so.

As I said at the start, I truly believe this is a direct result of unchecked stress and not paying attention to personal needs. More rest, less rage. Beware of those things we *have* to do that wear away our sensibilities. Find rest in between. And share the burden before it's too late.

 ## Checking the Margins

I hear it often, "The Lord never gives you more than you can handle." While it sounds spiritual on the surface, this sentiment is not at all biblical. We may very well have to deal with more than we can handle. Jesus Himself expressed that feeling (see Matthew 27:46). The verse of Scripture, from the Apostle Paul's own despair, that should replace that sentiment above can give a huge amount of encouragement:

> *For we do not want you to be unaware, brothers, of the affliction we experienced in Asia. For we were so utterly burdened beyond our strength that we despaired of life itself. Indeed, we felt that we had received the sentence of death. But that was to make us rely not on ourselves but on God who raises the dead. He delivered us from such a deadly peril, and he will deliver us. On him we have set our hope that he will deliver us again.*
> *(2 Corinthians 1:8–10)*

Paul reminds us we are not to rely on ourselves! When we feel we can't handle all we've been given, it may be absolutely so. We need God's hand to deliver us. We must lean on His love, His understanding, and take His yoke at all times. And note how honesty about our burden opens the way to hope.

You may need to take some time and consider where you are on the advocacy spectrum. Be honest with yourself.

Are you: Or:

Hiding at home......................Adventuring with your loved one?
Timid and subservient......................Courageous and Prepared?
Frustrated and bitter...........................Patient and full of Grace?

No matter where you are, it's okay. It's all part of the process of understanding what might be a new reality. Once you know where you are, you can then begin to move toward actions and attitudes that pull us out of depression and into victory.

 ## Pushing the Margins

Instead of sitting and waiting for the world to change, we can do a few things. These things should help us, and others, expand the understanding of our challenges. Do these and life will get a little easier.

1. Educate yourself so you can educate others.
2. Prioritize personal needs. This is where exercising grace will separate the *must do* from the *nice to have* and help you use your energy wisely.
3. Find partners. We were created for community.[19] Don't go it alone.
4. Celebrate every victory.
5. Never give up!

After considering all you have read and all you have personally experienced, you must know and prioritize your personal needs. We're not done though.

---

[19] See Hebrews 10:25, Colossians 3:13, Galatians 6:2, Proverbs 27:17

Your needs are just one layer of this big picture collage. There are other layers to add that we will look at next.

Let's talk about celebrating for a moment. Creating little goals gives us things to celebrate every day. You will have to remind yourself that we are trying to change the culture. We are attempting to change paradigms of how people think. That is a task that takes time, an immense amount of patience, and the need to persevere—unlike what most would ever need to endure otherwise. But you have the greater good at stake. You can rest assured your heavenly Father approves of all these efforts. The proof is in Scripture, and not only in Scripture, but the very words of Jesus.

The first time you are part of hosting an event with a meal, even if there is only one new family there, celebrate. You just acted on Luke 14:13–14. The first time you get a hug from a new friend with Down Syndrome at the water table of a 5K, celebrate. You just acted on Matthew 9:38. One day you will sit at a graduation and watch a young man with autism walk across that stage and proudly accept his diploma. You will hug his mom, knowing she never thought he would make it, and celebrate. After all, that family continued to press toward the goal, and God was with them too. Celebrate when any friend with a disability is included without the disability getting the unnecessary spotlight. As you push those margins, you will find many more reasons to celebrate!

Adjusting the Margins

So the goal is for all those challenges you have read about thus far to go away. The dream of every disability advocate is to advocate ourselves out of a job! We don't want to have to remind people why every human being deserves to be treated with dignity. We don't want to have to attend IEP meetings to remind officials of the law they are very familiar with yet are trying to avoid.

As we push on the margins that exist today, if we are diligent and never give up, there will be no choice but to adjust them to welcome everyone. We aren't there yet, but I am very confident our efforts will be rewarded, for God loves the weak, the poor, the lame, and the blind. May all we do be for the glory of God and His kingdom!

Chapter 5
Understanding Ministry

Pulling Back the Curtains of Ministry and Ministry Leadership

I have a crazy idea that each of us caring for a loved one with a disability can make this world a better place, not only as an advocate for education and our family life, but also for our faith community. It's a crazy idea because there is so much seemingly working against us. Respect for all human beings is still not guaranteed. Protecting the dignity of others is often an afterthought. And all too often a person's ability and worth is graded according to some ideal standard. Our faith communities are not immune to these problems. In fact, the problems are amplified because the church should be the one place that intentionally guards itself against those behaviors. Stories I've heard over and over suggest the church is not doing that well. This should not even be a thing we need to discuss. But here we are. When I am sitting at an information table that provides valuable suggestions many ignore, it makes me sad. I am sad because this is not how the Christian church should behave. The secular community is often doing a much better job of including our loved ones than the church. We must do better.

It is fascinating to me that my first inclination in attempting to address this problem was to ask, "How did we get here?" Why are seminaries not actively addressing this issue? Why are most churches exempt from ADA accessibility standards? There are rumors that faith organizations actually lobbied to be sure they did not have to comply. I classify it a rumor because a moderate internet search has yielded no proof. It may be my Google skills are weak on this subject. Regardless, one thing is certain, so many of our faith communities have not taken necessary steps to address ADA specific problem areas in their facilities.

To address the challenges, in this chapter I would like to pull back the curtain surrounding Christian ministry just a bit. My goal is to help us all empathize with what the ministry leader is dealing with on a regular basis. I want to be very clear to mention these should not be interpreted as excuses. There is no excuse for a family being turned away from a faith community. There are reasons, though, and we do well by first understanding them. I am convinced this little bit of insight will help us effect change with patience and grace.

With this information, you will be able to advocate for faith supports that help the church refocus on this population that is repeatedly denied a place at Christ's table. I expect your response to this information will be wholly unique from anyone else's. I believe that because we are all uniquely equipped with different gifts and different experiences that inform our actions. As you read, will you also be in prayer? Ask our heavenly Father how He wants you to use this information.

Is Everyone Really Oblivious?

Let's start with considering why Christian faith communities may be oblivious to the needs of people and families with disabilities. The most basic reason is lack of proximity to people who are different. At that first conference I attended in California, one of the speakers asked, "How many parents were told to put your child in an institution and start over?" The large number of hands that went up—wow. It made me want to cry. This wasn't 1950 or even 1980. This was 2002 and a large portion of those hands had children under the age of ten. For far too long our disabled children were sent away in order to relieve parents of the burden of care. And they were rarely seen in the community again.

Laws and expectations of care have changed and continue to change. Institutions are closing. There is a strong push toward community support. Unfortunately, so many communities and their secular and faith organizations are woefully unprepared to provide that support. Moving with the military provided a glimpse into the very different standards of support available across the United States. Even neighboring cities and counties can have very different ideas about support priorities. As a result, families choose to stay home, especially if their challenges seem invisible to others. The invisible challenges include those without external clues of medical equipment support, such as skull cap helmets, oxygen tanks, or wheelchairs. At first glance there might be no way to tell if someone needs extra support because there may be no immediate outward cue. My boys do not look disabled to most. It's not until someone tries to engage them in conversation that their autism is apparent.

If you really stop to think about it, why wouldn't those with big struggles stay home? Technology has reached a level we once only dreamed about or read in science fiction novels. From the comfort of home we can order groceries for delivery and avoid the judgmental, uncaring looks from complete strangers who assume that out-of-control child simply needs some discipline. The computer has become a gateway to social interaction and unlimited research. But is the computer really the lifesaver we think it is? Eventually we will realize that screens and keyboards are insufficient for our sanity.

As a champion for faith and family, we must understand that when we stay at home, we forfeit two opportunities. The first thing we forfeit is learning how to overcome the challenges that would otherwise prevent us from participating. If we never go to a restaurant, we will never learn how to compensate and have an enjoyable night. One of the greatest discussions I have had with one of Matthias' teachers was her telling me how proud she was to see us out at a restaurant the night before, and that she noticed how well behaved the boys were. I had no idea she was there. It felt so good to hear our hard work had paid off in the eyes of another. If we did not continue to try, we would never have learned the secrets to a successful dinner out with our boys.

When we stay home we also forfeit expecting others to be understanding and accommodating. It is absolutely unrealistic to expect everyone around you to be helpful when you are dealing with tough behaviors in public. Most do not understand what might be happening and will shy away. Others only know their own experiences with children and assume the behavior they see is a natural result of being spoiled. We simply do not live in a world where people consistently assume the best of others instead of the worst. It will be tough.

But we must be willing to face the challenges. Those who do not understand disabilities *need* us to model, encourage, or prod them in ways that will help them think and act in ways that move them beyond their own boundaries.

Every person we can educate may someday be an ally. And when we visit and participate in those places that do understand and accommodate the varied needs of others, we reward their efforts. We also show other patrons why those supports are needed.

How we attempt to function in our society is infinitely important. When you step out of your home, you are an advocate. Will you choose to advocate with patience or tension? Will you choose grace or victimhood? We also still live in a world where things we do not understand or even agree with can be threatening and frightening. When we step into the public, are we willing to educate and carry on, doing the best we can? Or do we storm out in a huff with hurt feelings because someone spoke an insensitive word? We can always hope there will be people in our midst with patience and a willingness to learn something new. Will you acknowledge that it will take time for others to retrain their thoughts concerning those with disabilities? You will overcome challenges when the attitude you present is one of patience and grace. Otherwise no one will listen.

So the answer to the question, "Is everyone really oblivious?" is: it depends. If a person has never had a direct and personal interaction with a disabled person and never had a conversation with someone about disability accommodations, then yes, they are oblivious—through no fault of their own. In the next section we will look at how to help everyone be aware.

Radars

While personally examining this issue, I realized we are dealing with what I will call "Radars and Rice Bowls." Both are familiar words that likely seem strange not only together, but in this context. Let me explain.

On ships of any large size, the control room has a station that displays information from the radar system of the locations of any other vessel or significant mass around them they should know about. Known vessels and hazards to navigation appear and disappear as they come in and out of sensor range. They also have other radar equipment which shows patterns of weather the vessel needs to be mindful of as they maneuver the waterway. Those two radar antennae are actively looking for very different information. Without these tools our waterways would be extremely dangerous places for vessels.

We all have a radar of sorts. We keep watch for things that are important to us. Our personal interests help our mind's eye find things that others may completely ignore. And I don't mean ignore in a bad way. Our mind filters out things it considers unnecessary. Early on, after my children were diagnosed, it was easy to see that disability awareness was simply not on my radar before then. So by extension, if it wasn't on my radar, how or why should I expect it to be on anyone else's? Without a family connection or other dramatic exposure to the issue, the world is blissfully unaware.

So what does the ministry leader radar look for? Ministry leaders generally work through five areas of concern. This isn't meant to cover everything, just those common in my experience:

◊   preaching/teaching,
◊   pastoral care,
◊   discipleship,
◊   missions of the church,
◊   general administration.

Once upon a time churches expected their staff to be able to do all five. Today, healthy churches try to be much more realistic with expectations and acknowledge which of the five areas ministry leaders do very well, and in which areas they need support.

Now imagine each of these ministry areas is like a radar screen. If the ministry leader is naturally gifted in pastoral care, his screen may look like this: Each blip on the radar is a family or individual. That larger dot represents the family that just lost a daughter unexpectedly. The dot in the top right is a military family that just moved back home and is struggling with PTSD. That cluster on the bottom left is the families in his small group pinned there permanently. The preaching/teaching radar might be looking for stories, analogies, resources and quotes. It is also looking for subjects that need to be addressed for the benefit of many. The administration radar might resemble a calendar superimposed with a color-coded to-do list based on who is responsible for the different tasks. As the days roll by, the focus changes based on what needs to be wrapped up versus what needs to get started.

Real life says they need to be mindful of all the different ministry areas, and so the different radar filters will overlap. Now the ministry leader has blips and bleeps alerting all over the place. Knowing this, what do you think happens when we come with the need to talk about disability issues? We know it is important for the church to be intentional about welcoming families with disability. If we frame the conversation as being about *missions*, and we are not talking to the person who primarily thinks about missions, that person will not process it well nor quickly. It does not fit on any of their radar screens naturally, so it will take more effort to get the point across.

But what if we frame the conversation within the context of pastoral care to the pastor who is most gifted in that area? Now we're talking a similar language. There is a much greater chance the pastor's mental "software" will update, and the radar will start picking up on those needs and adding them to the priority list. Oh, did we know that Donna stopped coming to church because she is caring for her mom who fell and broke her hip and they can't get to the sanctuary because of our stairs? Or what about Richard, who loves to sing but whose failing eye sight doesn't let him read the words on the screen anymore, and he often leaves the service sad and frustrated instead of fulfilled? If you are able to understand your ministry leaders on this level, it will help you be a better partner in ministry.

Rice Bowls

Imagine with me that the ministry leader has prepared their lunch just as they do every afternoon in a small bowl, mostly full of rice. Here we come with an idea, let's call it a nice twelve-ounce steak cooked to perfection. To the ministry leader that has never had a steak with rice; it may seem too big or completely unnecessary. "This rice is just fine without that." And within the context of ministry, the limited time, money, and human resources are already stretched thin. No one is disputing its value, but it's not rice, and it is certainly too big for this bowl.

I have heard this analogy used twice. The first time was to justify why we could not do something new. The second was in conversation about trying to figure out whom to approach with a new idea.

Much like understanding a ministry leader's radar—we also need to understand their rice bowl. If you are part of a small church, you cannot assume the pastor is the only resource. Do you have elders or other lay ministry leaders who are responsible for leading and guiding in certain areas? Medium to large church staffs are usually clear about their division of responsibilities. Be sure you talk to the right person. For those focused on doing a few things well, where they have clear boundaries defining their work, anything beyond that scope is too much and won't be considered. If it isn't "rice" it doesn't belong.

The rice bowl analogy is the one I see played out in initial meetings. New ideas or needs are often too much for them to consume. Your idea may be too big for their budgets, for their limited volunteer base, or for their overextended staff to adopt. The whole atmosphere of the room becomes heavy. As an advocate you will come across the seemingly insurmountable brick wall barriers as ministry leaders attempt to protect their schedules. They cannot imagine adding anything else to the bowl that is already filled to the brim and in danger of spilling. You must be strong and approach it as if you are adding soy sauce or brown sugar. The rice will be better with this addition and "taste" like ministry as Christ intends.

With these two analogies in mind, let's look at how I think we got here. I believe the ministry leader has three significant forces working to dictate their priorities: education, experience, and workload. In truth, all of us function under these influences.

For those who knew their calling early on, their education will have a definitive impact on their ministry foundations. There may have been an influential professor or a class that helped cement their attitude on many subjects. If our seminaries miss discussing disabilities, and their impact and contribution to ministry, those students won't know to look for them. Many have never been exposed to the unique needs of so many individuals in their academic studies, and so they are completely oblivious.

Some never receive a formal education with cap and gown and diploma, and therefore experience has been their best teacher. This ministry leader may attend conferences and connect with social media think tanks. Common sense and key resources have been their guides as they maneuver through the joys and challenges each week. Whether the church is large or small, the challenges in front of them dictate how time is spent any given week. They may know that members have hearing challenges but do not understand the church's responsibility to be sure they can hear during the service.

The force of experience then leads us to workload. Do you have a part-time, bi-vocational ministry leader still expected to do everything a full-time minister would? Was the children's director hired to work twenty hours a week yet expected to do all the same events as the last full-time director? Your associate minister may be the one to work with you on preparing the church to be more welcoming, but be aware. He or she may also be responsible for finances and organizing small groups, and the welcome ministry, and whatever else is identified as a priority.

The point is that we need to be fully aware of the forces working against us. There is usually no malice or intentionality by anyone to missing those with disabilities. They simply do not realize what is missing. Once they are made aware, they must update their "radar" software or decide that their rice will taste much better with steak and soy sauce added. And then we must be willing to step up as a partner and help figure out how we make it all work.

Demands of the Ministry

Have you thought much about what demands your ministry leader's time and energy? Obvious things include such as study time, planning, administration, and counseling. Another curtain we need to peek behind is what I will call the "busy closet." This closet has all those other things that we generally do not see our ministry leaders dealing with that actually take an exorbitant amount of their week.

We acknowledge the need for a pastor to study and prepare for next week's sermon or lesson. Do they also do any of these?

◊ Meetings with staff, with the leadership team, with the church lay leaders, with the finance team, with the outreach team, with _____

◊ Pastoral counseling. This is a natural duty of our ministry leaders who are gifted shepherds.

◊ Crisis Calls and Emergencies. When there is an accident, often the church/ministry leader is one of the first to know, depending on the church culture.

◊ Pray with the seniors. Is it once a week? Once a month? The pastor may be expected to be there to pray with them and speak to the group.

◊ Visit shut-ins and the sick. This likely takes more of their time than one might realize.

◊ Prayer networking. This may be a partial recharge time where they connect with other pastors to pray for self, their church body, and the community.

◊ School assemblies. Does your ministry leader go to the school performances, the awards assembly, or even show up to have lunch at school with the students in the cafeteria?

◊ Weddings and funerals. This too can gobble more time than we realize especially if there is premarital counseling happening.

◊ Family priorities. This one really isn't optional as family time supports a healthy minister, but for some reason we tend to forget they also need personal time.

With all these other tasks that may be happening throughout the week, please be sure to make an appointment when you are ready to have this conversation. Your pastor may have an open door policy, but an appointment with at least an hour block of time means you will have their undivided attention. If they are mentally able to prepare for your conversation, you will have a better chance of having their full attention.

When I need to talk to my husband about important things, I have to be sure he isn't in another "box."[20] If he is currently working on a project, I let him finish before asking him to think about and process something new. If I don't do that, he won't participate well in the conversation, and it will only end in frustration.

Now consider walking into your pastor's office, not understanding he needs to walk out the door in thirty minutes. He may have even mentioned he only has a half hour but still wants to honor your visit. Do you think he is really able to focus on what you are saying? He may try his hardest, but realize the mind may be wandering to prepare for getting out the door and making sure he doesn't forget anything.

Your Church Culture

You may have read the previous section thinking, "That doesn't happen in my church." It is quite possible your church culture is very different and not nearly as hectic or the ministry leader's week is not at all as intense as what I described. There may still be a schedule though, and commitments unique to your ministry staff that you would be wise to acknowledge and steer around.

---

[20] There are some very fun online videos about the difference between men's brains and women's brains. You should check them out. Look for Mark Gundor or Joe McGee.

Timing

Along with understanding how our ministry leaders are engaged each week, we all need to fully understand the power of the calendar. Holidays and major events are dictators for most church staff. We must consider that up to four weeks before a major event, the week following, and the months of March, April, November, and December are really bad times to try starting a conversation on anything new and important.

Have you ever planned a big event? As the big day creeps closer and closer, the anxiety level may rise. And what if the success of the event might have an impact on your continued employment? Big events, especially if there are lots of moving parts to be managed, may cause the leaders to put blinders on as soon as three to four weeks out but definitely a week or two before.

Holy days can be demanding. Every small group wants their pastor to come to their party. Gifts to shut-ins need to be delivered. Study time has likely increased, and the already packed calendar has no wiggle room. Which holidays require extra community events or special services? Our faith holidays are not days of rest for our ministry leaders.

Keep watch of your church calendar. Be sure you aren't introducing new things too close to major events. If you must say something, be sure you acknowledge it may not be the best time and ask to get on someone's calendar in the near future.

Being a Partner

I need to emphasize again the need to be a partner in these efforts. We may have to roll up our sleeves and help get efforts up and moving. We cannot expect to walk into an office, leave all the work to do on the pastor's desk, and walk away.

When talking to the pastor, our primary objective is awareness and understanding. This will also be true for any conversation with support staff, an elder or deacon body, a church board, or other group responsible for vetting ministries.

In an ideal situation we will not be the person responsible for coordinating the very efforts we need to be participating in for any great length of time. It may be, though, we have to help get things started. If that happens, remember to find those partners and slowly inch your way out of leadership responsibilities.

We may have to shadow our child for a few weeks on Sunday morning until a buddy system is established. We may have to meet with staff and volunteers regularly to brainstorm ideas. Throughout the whole process we will need a lot of patience and grace as everyone is learning.

Checking the Margins

Every church is different. We should not assume every ministry leader is wrestling with all the things I have listed.

But does any of it match?

Is it possible we need to take a hard look at the demands we put on staff and lay leaders that have nothing to do with reaching people for Christ?

Are you prepared to jump into the mix to help get a conversation started and help encourage action?

Checking the margins is all about analyzing where we are and where we would like to be. Once you answer those questions you may need the information coming up to create the strategies to push on those margins.

We will overcome
challenges when the
attitude we present
is one of patience
and grace.

Chapter 6
Helping the Church Understand

It's time! You've checked the calendar, consulted with the secretary, and prayed for grace and wisdom to talk with the pastor about doing some things differently. But how do you start? In this section we will explore the things you may need to help the church understand.

Statistics and Souls

We cannot fully grasp why this conversation is so important without looking at statistics. In the United States, the census bureau takes the information they collect every ten years, and it is sorted and analyzed for many different purposes. One of those analyses shows the percentages of our population that is disabled down to the type of disability and age ranges. There are very detailed reports for your state and even your locality. Today's statistics tell us:

1 in 59 has Autism.[21]

10 percent of US adults have trouble seeing (even with corrective lenses)[22]

1 in 5 of the overall US Population is disabled.[23]

These three figures cover a wide spectrum of challenges, but they are still challenges nonetheless. While our secular society has been forced to think about some of these challenges and ensure public spaces are accessible, that is not the case for many locations and especially in most houses of worship. While ADA[24] laws may have been adhered to, when done at the minimum, barriers to access still exist for many.

There are faces and souls behind those numbers— not only the disabled but also their caregivers and family members. Those families know all about the barriers that keep them from going to certain restaurants or even church. A faith family must have

---

[21] https://www.cdc.gov/ncbddd/autism/data.html

[22] http://www.afb.org/info/blindness-statistics/2

[23] https://www.census.gov/newsroom/releases/archives/miscellaneous/cb12-134.html

[24] ADA stands for the Americans with Disabilities Act passed in 1990. It affords similar protections against discrimination to Americans with disabilities_as the Civil Rights Act of 1964, which made discrimination based on race, religion, sex, national origin, and other characteristics illegal. In addition, unlike the Civil Rights Act, the ADA also requires covered employers to provide reasonable accommodations to employees with disabilities, and imposes accessibility requirements on public accommodations.

room for them. If a congregation does not have a process, or at least readiness, for welcoming and accommodating the needs of individuals, everyone is missing out on the full experience of the faith community.

So how do we change the endings of countless stories heard over and over of churches unable to include families with disabilities?

◊ Ask God to lead you to the church He intends for you.
◊ Commit to advocate.
◊ Commit to support the work ahead as much as possible with clear boundaries of expectations on your involvement.

You may have to help the staff and congregation understand what the church is missing. If you met with the pastor tomorrow, would you know what to say? Familiarize yourself with these talking points to help them understand a few things such as:

◊ Who are we talking about?
◊ What are the barriers we need to pull down?
◊ Why is any of this important anyway?
◊ How does our theology impact this conversation?
◊ How can the church make a difference?

Whom Are We Talking About?

So whom are we talking about? We are talking about anyone struggling with differences in ability that limits or excludes them from participation with their peers at any level. This is a condition of life we usually refer to as being disabled.

Disability has two definitions:[25] 1) Lack of adequate power, strength, or physical or mental ability; incapacity. 2) A physical or mental handicap, especially one that prevents a person from living a full, normal life, or from holding a gainful job.

There's another word we should look up— handicap. It has four definitions:[26] 1) A race or other contest in which certain disadvantages or advantages of weight, distance, time, etc., are placed upon competitors to equalize their chances of winning. 2) The disadvantage or advantage itself. 3) Any disadvantage that makes success more difficult. 4) (Sometimes offensive) A physical or mental disability making participation in certain of the usual activities of daily living more difficult.

Our definitions of disability are important to note. Did you notice there must be a marker that determines if one is disabled or not? That marker cannot be considered absolute, though. The first definition

---

[25] From www.dictionary.com
[26] ibid

describes it as "a lack of ability." The next question we must then ask is, "compared to what?" Am I disabled because I can't open a pickle jar? Is that really a good definition? Moving to the second definition we are given some specifics but we are still searching for the comparison point. What truly is a "full, normal life?" Isn't it possible that any individual, irrespective of their abilities, can lead a full life? Isn't it a matter of personal perspective? We will explore how, with the proper support, anyone can lead a full and normal life. *Normal* is far too subjective to be a factor.

Words on paper are one thing, but what about the souls these words describe, such as the child who has never built a sandcastle on the beach because the wheelchair can't get through the sand? Or maybe it's the mom who hasn't had a personal day in months because she has no one she can trust to watch her daughter. It's the father who can't get past the idea his boy isn't going to play football because of a heart condition. It's the teen girl who just found out she'll never be able to dance again because of injuries from a car accident. It's the family who hasn't taken a vacation in years because cancer treatments have used up all their days off and all their savings.

On and on we could go describing the 20 percent of the population the US Census Bureau tallied as disabled in 2010.[27] Many are born this way. Others are victims of trauma. Stop for a moment and consider the effects of the natural aging process. Our hearing may diminish, requiring an aide to amplify the sounds around us. Hips will stop moving, causing debilitating pain, demanding a surgical procedure and therapeutic rehabilitation. Memories may be hard to find and faces difficult to recognize. It should be a somewhat sobering thought to acknowledge we will all one day be disabled in some way if we stay on this earth long enough.

So, let's go back to the 20 percent number. We may have to ask our ministry leader a question such as: If we were to stand in the sanctuary and look out on the people, would you be able to say the assembly reflects the statistic? That number does include those with limited mobility, hearing loss, and other age-related challenges, so the answer may be yes. The next question must then be: Are we as a church body supporting those needs? Is it possible that those with limited vision, for example, sit in silent frustration because they can't read the words to the songs anymore? Is everyone aware of the hearing supports available? We may have to help the ministry leader take an extra hard look at the barriers that prevent inclusion.

---

[27] Americans with Disabilities, 2010.
https://www.census.gov/content/dam/Census/library/publications/2012/demo/p70-131.pdf

The ministry leader may be interested in the "expectations and abilities" worksheet available at www.marginsofgrace.com/resources. This worksheet is intended to help ministry leaders and their worship teams verify if their expectations are actually matching experiences.

Barriers to Inclusion

"Walk a mile in my shoes." This old saying is usually a quick way to suggest you really have no idea what a person is going through or why they do what they do unless you've experienced life as they have. Consider those who are colorblind. For those who are not color blind, we can only imagine what it's like to live in a gray world. Do we do anything that requires someone to be able to see color to participate? How many card games do we play that depend on color matching? Is it possible your friend doesn't play because of reasons beyond not wanting to?

If you have surgery on your foot and have to use a wheelchair for a month, would you be able to go out with friends next week to your favorite hangout spot? Would you be able to get to the sanctuary at church? Would you have to sit in the aisle or in the back potentially impeding the flow of foot traffic?

Do you know anyone who has lived through a stroke? The lingering effects of that medical trauma may impact so many functions we take for granted. The mind may desire to speak but has forgotten how to make it happen.

Or what about the local soldier hero just home from war? He's received awards and medals for bravery and courage. Yet he rarely leaves his home now because of haunting images and sounds that tell him he is never safe. The threats of improvised explosive devices are everywhere. His post-traumatic stress is crippling, he has a hard time being around people, and not even his faith seems to be able to make it better.

There are barriers to inclusion most do not understand exist. Every one of these conditions I have mentioned is experienced by a minority of people and may be rare or unusual. When a minority of the population experiences these challenges, it should not surprise us that accommodations are uncommon. As advocates, we can work toward making certain accommodations standard instead of exceptional. There are five types of barriers but we will address three of them here: architecture, communication, and attitude. The other two barriers they will need to know about are programmatic and liturgical. You can read more about all the barriers in Erik Carter's book, Including People with Disabilities in Faith Communities. It's a great resource.

Architecture

Architecture here addresses the physical traits of the building that could be barriers. In the hierarchy of difficulty, architecture is the simplest, albeit perhaps the highest impact on dollars, to overcome. Usually this includes steps, the width of doorways, the size of restrooms, even the size of individual restroom stalls. Without significant help from others, can everyone get to all the spaces where people are gathered? If Joe teenager in a wheelchair has to be carried up a flight of stairs by two men to get to the youth room, the architecture is a barrier. If Sally has to go outside and come around to access the fellowship hall, the architecture is a barrier. If your guest preacher on Sunday morning has to speak from the floor of the sanctuary because he can't navigate the steps to the pulpit area, the architecture is a barrier.

Some would refute calling these barriers. "It's no problem to help Joe to his classroom." "Sally can still get to the hall." "We move the microphone around all the time."

All those things may be true; however, for Sally, people forget this route around the building does not have an awning. What about when it is raining or even snowing? Is Sally truly valued as an indispensable member of the body of Christ like everyone else? Doesn't Sally deserve a warm, indoor path to the fellowship hall traveling with everyone else? Of course she does. It's a barrier that needs to be addressed. Architecture changes support everyone. We should just expect there will be those that need these supports among us. The body of Christ includes the strong and the weak. As the Apostle Paul writes,

> *On the contrary, the parts of the body that seem weaker are indispensable, and on those parts of the body that we think less honorable we bestow the greater honor, and our unpresentable parts are treated with greater modesty, which our more presentable parts do not require. (1 Corinthians 12:22–24)*

Communication

The next easiest is the communication barrier. Compared to the others, it is the broadest in its scope. It includes things we do for all, but also requires attention to individual needs. It covers the language we use during our service times at church. It's the words we choose when a mom comes to pick up her child from the nursery. It's the ways we help or hinder those with speech or hearing impairments. If the volume is so high it hurts their bones, with no quieter area to retreat to, they likely won't stay. Did you know that bulletins are still very valuable tools for those who are new or like to know order of events? A picture schedule in a classroom helps children know exactly what they are doing while there and helps decrease their anxiety. Does your child or loved one use any special fidgets or aids to help them stay focused or calm at school or day support? Those same tools would be useful to have available during any church gathering. This is just a small sample of areas the communication barrier covers.

The key to overcoming this barrier lies in a commitment by everyone to identify and address any communication issue that arises that may keep someone away. Are we willing to ask our people if we could do some things better? Are we willing to read books and apply the concepts we learn? Are we willing to make volunteer training mandatory so everyone is comfortable and prepared for whoever comes through the door? How does the ministry team greet each challenge? The way we respond to a disabled individual or their caregiver will reflect our commitment to love our neighbor as ourselves.

> And [Jesus] said to him, "You shall love the Lord your God with all your heart and with all your soul and with all your mind. This is the great and first commandment. And the second is like it, You shall love your neighbor as yourself." (Matthew 22:37–39)

What if on Mother's Day, the staff picked a lovely video with beautiful scenic views and encouraging words for moms that flashed silently across the screen? There are likely a good number of older moms who would completely miss the message because they could not see the screens well enough. By choosing media that interacts with only one of our senses, we deny those without that sense from participating. Or what about the grandfather bound to a wheelchair? When the worship leader simply says, "Please stand to worship," he has excluded Granddad. Did he mean to exclude? Surely not! But he excluded nonetheless. Without consciously choosing to be more accommodating or deciding to use language that includes everyone, these unintended exclusions will continue. For a deeper exploration of this topic, consider reading <u>Accessible Gospel, Inclusive Worship</u> by Barbara Newman.

The Body of Christ must be intentional about communicating Christ's love—welcoming everyone, no matter the challenges they bring. Only then can we know we love one another as Christ called us to love.

Attitude

The biggest barrier of all to overcome is attitude. When talking about the subject of including people with disabilities to groups of people such as therapists and parents, I ask for their help in naming some of the challenges they have experienced trying to attend a church. Each challenge always falls within one of these three barrier categories. The category that always gets the most hits is attitude.

Those attitude hits usually manifest in frowns and judgmental side-eyed looks. It's the usher who thinks a child looking at an electronic device (even without sound) during worship is distracting or inappropriate. It's the Sunday school teacher who can't understand why a child can't sit with everyone else during the lesson.

When we do not stop and consider individual needs, we add to the attitude barrier. Attitude barriers seem to be rooted in the unknown. The unknown makes us uneasy. Being uneasy is never desired, and we usually do all we can to stop the feeling. The easiest way is to remove ourselves from the offending source. The unknown can also arouse fear of inadequacy. Feeling inadequate is especially troublesome when we have a responsibility to others. We don't want to fall short or mess up, so our default mode is to avoid. I see it all the time.

I believe breaking down this barrier requires two basic things: experience and empathy.

We conquer the unknown with experience. Some think experience means education, and while that might help, it won't be as effective as real-life experience. Reading books and watching videos may help us some, but they are no substitute for genuine connections. We need to interact with people who are disabled. More than that, though, we need to get to know them as *people* not as a *disability*. What are their hopes and dreams? What do they like to do the most? What is their favorite afternoon activity?

To find this interaction, consider going and cheering for the athletes during the next Special Olympics games. Those are family members and their friends in the stands next to you. Strike up a conversation. How about sponsoring a water stop during the next walk/run charity 5K in your region? Encourage and support their efforts just because it's a good thing to do. What about volunteering at the adult day care center on the other side of town? You just might find a friend who loves to play checkers as much as you do. Does your church visit a convalescent home? How many of the residents are not elderly? Those younger residents are likely there because they have a disability that won't allow them to live on their own, which also likely means they don't have any family nearby. What kind of adventures could you share while getting to know that person?

The other key to breaking the attitude barrier is empathy. We must be very careful to consider the needs of others and not think so highly of ourselves, for we are all temporarily abled. Medical advances help us live longer, but knees and hips still give out. Hearing and sight still diminish. A car accident can send the track star to rehab and a wheelchair for months, if not permanently.

For the longest time my education suggested, and I believed, that success in ministry was rooted first in a solid vision for the church; second, a rallying mission; and third, shared values. However, I have recently heard a different theory that suggests our shared values are the number one indicator of ministry success. The best vision and mission plan will always fail if values are not shared by all. What do we value? What matters most to our staff? Do we have empathy for and value all people? Do we truly believe Scripture? Can we grasp that the mandate Jesus himself gave His people in Luke 14 is also for us?

> *When you give a feast, invite the poor, the crippled, the lame, the blind, and you will be blessed, because they cannot repay you. (Luke 14:13–14a)*

How many do we invite to the table that have no way of contributing or returning the favor? Do we take the time to truly invite them to be a part of the body of Christ, or do we give them a bag of groceries and send them on their way, pleased we have done our part?

As a champion for faith and family trying to help ministry leaders understand, sharing these three barriers is a good start.

Why it is Important

Heed a word of caution here before we dive into the *why* of this conversation. You may be tempted to think you know why and can skip this section. Please don't do that. There is a great big picture being painted here, and you don't want to punch a hole in the canvas.

The *why* is deeper than you think. We assume it's because "God says so" or "the Bible says so." If that were sufficient, this book wouldn't be necessary. If that were sufficient, my family would have never experienced the challenges searching for a church the way we did.

***

Imagine for a moment walking through a pair of glass doors into a medium sized room just as the sun is coming up. The doors open freely from the outside, but you are startled by the echo of a locking sound when they close. Uh oh. There is no handle to open the door from the inside! Peering back through the glass and knocking on the door proves fruitless as there is no one out there.

Turning away from the door you hear faint sounds of conversation, and a classical music station plays softly in the background. Folks of all ages are seated in small clusters around the room. Everyone seems consumed with their little conversations, and no one notices you wandering among them. Just then a wide-eyed gal from around a corner runs past you toward the door.

"No! No, I missed it again," she shouts. "I know I heard this door open!" She frantically looks left and right, hoping someone is still close by. Seeing no one, she slowly sulks to the floor with hands and cheek pressed firmly to the glass.

Finally she looks up and toward you. "You just got here, didn't you?" The sadness and subdued tone of her voice sends a chill down your spine. "And you don't even know where you are."

She's right.

"Welcome to your new reality," as she spreads her arms wide. "The world has exiled you here because you or your family doesn't fit in anymore. Therapists will rule your schedule. Most of your friends will fade away because you're too hard to deal with. Your disabled child is now your full-time job. And believe it or not, your church will disregard you. They can't help anymore. Pastors will pass by this door and never open it for you no matter how hard you pound. I know. I've tried. And so have they." A wide sweeping gesture with both hands towards the clusters of quiet chatter ends with a loud sigh before she pulls herself back to her feet.

***

So many times I've felt like the wide-eyed gal frantically hoping for someone to come along and open that door. Sitting in a musty nursery week after week with my newborn all by myself sent me through those glass doors. I was separated from church life, separated from the body of believers, because my child had unusual needs. The world was just beginning to identify those needs, so it's not surprising there would be lag time with awareness, but here we are more than twenty years later, and the one-way glass doors still exist.

***

Let's take this imagery a step further.

All the folks in this room have a personal relationship with Christ. They likely had a salvation experience as a child and know the light outside is their hope. We can glean a little of that hope by staying as close to the door as possible. Every so often a chair will go flying toward the door, in someone's hope of breaking out. But it stands firm.

***

I knew and understood the need for a faith community, yet never wanted to show up unannounced. So a phone call to a new church was my attempt to break down those glass doors. I attended support groups, hoping to find someone with a church community but no one had one. So the frustration would build and depression would deepen.

***

Let's take this analogy one last step further still. Off this main room are hallways that seem to go on forever. There is no electricity in this concrete brick building, so the only light is coming from the glass doors. As expected, the farther down the hall one goes, the darker it gets. And there are rooms all down these halls. The little LED flashlight from my key ring shows me there are people in these rooms too! They're sitting in complete darkness. They have been here so long they don't even know where the door is. They know of nothing that can help them and are certain there is no such thing as God. How could there be?

***

These are the outcasts of our society. They're the distractions, the interruptions, the needy that demand so much of our time and resources. I know that working with people with challenges is difficult. I also know that if we are serious about reflecting Christ in our every day, we must figure out how to look beyond the difficulty.

> *When He saw the crowds, he had compassion for them, because they were harassed and helpless, like sheep without a shepherd. Then he said to his disciples, "The harvest is plentiful, but the laborers are few; therefore pray earnestly to the Lord of the harvest to*

send out laborers into his harvest.
(Matthew 9:36–38)

Prepare to Answer Questions

I realize I may be in the minority here, but my biggest concern for my children after their diagnosis was not their future. It was their eternity. I was raised in a denomination that required a verbal confession of faith of one's own free will to enter the Kingdom of Heaven. There seemed to be exceptions for infants and toddlers who had not reached the age of accountability, but no one really ever talked much about that until faced with such a loss.

Enter two little ones who cannot engage in a conversation. As far as we could tell, these boys would never be able to even understand the concept of a creator God, much less verbalize trust in a living Savior. "Doesn't that mean…" I could not reconcile the obvious conclusion in my brain.

When talking with a pastor or chaplain about this issue, the usual response was, "Oh, you don't need to worry about your boys. They'll be fine." Such responses were infuriating. So you've preached and taught that only a personal verbal confession of faith unlocks that eternal relationship, but my sons are exempt? And you're not going to even explain why that is? Blah, blah, age of accountability, blah, blah, blah. He might as well have been a grown-up as depicted in a classic Peanuts cartoon trying to give that explanation. It did not survive the wash.

This issue is a big part of the conversations I have with ministry leaders. Our ministry leaders need to be prepared to answer questions. Caregivers need answers to tough questions, and in every possible way, they must be answered with Scripture and a sound interpretation thereof. To tell a mom, "Don't worry about it," is condescending and a cop-out. It may satisfy some, but it wasn't enough for me, and I must expect I am not alone in this.

Our family members with significant cognitive differences may never be able to express themselves like most and therefore never be able to fulfill the requirements so many denominations espouse. Some parents will understand that to mean their child will have no chance of eternity with Christ. It may even be enough to cause a complete spiritual breakdown.

My own family's understanding of this issue is now rooted in a Reformed understanding of the covenant relationship we have with Christ. You may have a Wesleyan or Roman Catholic or Orthodox understanding. Each of us must come to grips with this issue within our own understanding or faith tradition. If you are interested in what my family believes, you can find it in the extras on page 163. I will, however, share one experience along this line of understanding.

Communion and the Disabled: A Personal Revelation

Through twists and turns of divine providence we found the denomination we knew would lead us to our local church home. Finally, the whole family—all four of us—were sitting in worship together! This was a big deal. By this time the boys were in their mid-to-late teens. Everyone welcomed us with so much love. It was wonderful.

Attending church those first few weeks was great. The boys sat very nicely through the entirety of each service. Each child got a dollar of his own to put in the offering plate. They stood nicely with us when Scripture was being read. During the music, the youngest was even trying to sing along. No one seemed to be bothered by their occasional noises. Wow, this was going so well. It was such a blessing. It was really looking like we would be able to do this!

Then came Communion Sunday. Finally we get to participate in the Lord's Supper! Now remember, my husband and I had not regularly sat in worship together for about fifteen years. And neither child knew Christ personally as far as we knew. Therefore, they were not supposed to participate. It was my understanding that only those who had made a personal profession of faith were allowed at the communion table. So imagine my horror when the plate of bread was passed and I watched my husband take a piece for Joshua also. In that moment my eyes got wide and my heart rate increased to unhealthy levels and in my mind I was screaming, *No, no, no! What are you doing?* all in the span of four seconds as the plate was being passed. My husband never did make eye contact with me. He must have known I was dying inside, though, as the look on his face was very matter-of-fact, seemingly ignoring my internal conniption. Following his lead, I reluctantly allowed the youngest to take a piece before passing the plate along. And I repeated the words every person before me had said, "The body of Christ broken for you."

I was not at all of calm spirit as we took the bread element that morning. In the lull before the tray of cups arrived, I secretly desired a sinkhole to open up beneath me and suck me through. No one else needed to come, just me. Allowing the boys to participate was against the rules that would bring judgement on us both! But it was something my husband and I never discussed. It never occurred to me to have that conversation. I really thought we had a general understanding, but on that day, I was proven wrong.

My longed-for sinkhole didn't appear. There was nothing I could do now. Calm started to return, and I know the Holy Spirit was working with me. When the tray of cups arrived, the youngest eagerly took one and in order to encourage him to hold onto it and wait until everyone had been served, I once again repeated the words everyone else had said before me, "The blood of Christ shed for you." And then I repeated the phrase and made it personal. "The blood of Christ shed for you, Matthias." As soon as I said his name, I was completely awash with emotion. I am certain in that moment that I heard the words, "Yes it was. Matthias is welcome at My table." I could hardly keep myself together. Matthias looked at me with great concern as I started sobbing deeply, and I had to work very hard to compose myself. Of course, Christ died for my children too. They are welcome at God's table.

Now before you call me a heretic, I invite you to look at three tables in Scripture. The first is found in 2 Samuel 9, and the other two in Luke 14. Our Old Testament table tells us the story of King David and Mephibosheth. After he had gotten settled, David asked his servants if there was any of Saul's family left to whom he could show kindness. There was one, Jonathan's son, whom we are told was lame in both feet. Upon being summoned to the palace, Mephibosheth fell before the King and asked, "What is your servant, that you should look upon such a dead dog as I?" (NKJV)

King David then informed the servants that they would serve and care for Mephibosheth and "he shall eat at my table like one of the king's sons."

The second and third tables are found in Luke 14. With the first, Jesus himself is talking about what we should do when we give a dinner or a supper.

> *Do not ask your friends, or your brothers or relatives...lest they also invite you back, and you be repaid. But when you give a feast, invite the poor; the maimed, the lame, the blind. And you will be blessed, because they cannot repay you. (Luke 14: 13–14)*

Immediately after that talk, Luke gives us his version of Jesus' Parable of the Great Supper. The master was ready to begin, but all those who were originally invited were too busy doing other things. So the master sent his servants out to "bring in the poor and the maimed and the lame and the blind." He even said, "Compel them to come in," (Luke 14:23).

I realize the banquet table and the Lord's Table are different, but to a struggling family, they are more alike than not. Those with disabilities could easily still describe themselves as "less than a dead dog," because of how society sees them.

The absolute horror I felt because of my upbringing and the subsequent personal revelation I received might suggest we need to reconsider some things. Could it be that we have created rules and stumbling blocks for some individuals that Jesus never intended? How does Scripture and what it tells us about Jesus' actions inform the answers to this question?

How Can the Church Make a Difference?

Throughout this section we have been referring to things you may have to help the church understand. We now have to talk about how all this understanding will pragmatically help the church make a difference in the lives of families dealing with a disability. This is where what we have been talking about now grows wings, and we take off. Moving from knowledge to action is not always a reality, so stick with me.

There is one overarching principle for the rest of this discussion: Include everyone.

Include Everyone

There is one phrase we must all learn in order to be able to welcome everyone. "I don't really know _____, but let's figure it out." I don't know how to help Susie learn the Lord's Prayer, but let's figure it out. I don't know how we are going to get Matthew up the stairs to the classroom, but let's figure out a way to move the class. I don't really know why Jackson's PTSD keeps him from church, but let's figure out a way to bring church to Jackson.

Instead of saying, "Sorry we can't because _____,"
we need our ministry leaders to be willing to figure it
out. This is not only true regarding people with
disabilities; effective ministry leaders must apply this
mindset to everything they do in ministry. This kind of
commitment will also pave the way for our
congregations to be more reflective of our communities.
When we do that, we will reach our communities
better—and isn't that what every church wants? We
won't need an in-depth conference on stepping over
barriers, because we finally recognize them along the
way as just challenges to overcome.

Persevere

As an advocate you must accept that "include
everyone" is easy to say and yet tough to do. After all,
there is so much vying for priority attention. I hope you
will not be too disappointed when I tell you I cannot
give a list of steps beyond this point, because this
journey will be different for every advocate and every
church. God has granted you gifts and abilities He will
use to further His kingdom. The body of believers He
places you within will also have a unique culture and a
specific job to do in the community. No matter the
context though, people with disabilities should always
be included. Let's look again at the Scriptures that
motivate this work:

1 Corinthians 12 – Break down barriers that tell someone they are worthless.

Matthew 22 – Love one another as God loves us.

Luke 14: 21–24 – Compel them to come in.

Matthew 28:18–20 – Go, make disciples, baptize, teach.

Matthew 9:35–38 – The harvest is plentiful, but the laborers are few.

You might want to pick a couple and write them on your bathroom mirror. Choose one to tape to your steering wheel; maybe put one across the top of your computer monitor. Scripture is our motivator. You may think it's your experience, but it's not. Experience was just the vessel that led to the understanding of Scripture. People may be able to debate and cast doubt on an experience. But the Word of God is pretty clear about how we should treat those with disabilities.

Do you remember reading in Chapter 4 about "chaining?" I'll recap here. Chaining is a system of breaking down a direction into the mini tasks required to actually do the intended task. Remember considering all the little steps required to get a glass of milk? Okay, so your church needs to analyze where they are today, compare it to where they would like to be, and do some chaining to map out the steps.

Be aware: That chaining step may not include you! You must guard your heart against owning this process.

When we own a process, we naturally end up needing to control it. We do not want to control *anything* that belongs to God. And this task of inclusion certainly applies.

Also be aware that it may not go as fast as you think it should. It may not go as smoothly as it could. We need to ask God what exactly our involvement going forward looks like and be willing to obey, even if that means moving to another church and starting again. It could be your job is to simply plant a seed. Commitment and persistence are important. But do not attempt to do anything against the will of God; including staying somewhere when He has said, go. If things are just not moving, ask God again if this church is the right place for you. Personal experience says that if the inclusion you are looking for is not part of God's plan for that place and that time, it won't happen likely because there is a plan for your family elsewhere. We must be very careful to avoid judging when things do not happen as we think they should. No matter how hard we work, we must be sure we are doing the Lord's will in the right place and at the right time.

Please, *do not do this alone!* At the end of chapter four there is a list of steps in the Pushing the Margins review. If you need a step-by-step checklist, that would be it. But did you notice "find partners" is number two? Trying to do this alone is, well, lonely, and makes us vulnerable to attacks and temptations to give up.

With your partners:

◊ Pray for guidance and wisdom.

◊ Research the right people on staff to connect with. Your church secretary or a ministry assistant is a great place to start asking around.

◊ Pray more, especially for never ending grace toward those who need to understand.

◊ Choose the timing wisely. Check and confirm calendars.

◊ Meet with at least two people, perhaps the most appropriate ministry leader and an elder, deacon, or board member. This ensures that after your meeting the ministry leader has someone else to talk to who received the same information.

◊ Pray. Pray without ceasing. Pray about when and how to follow up after a meeting. Prayer keeps us connected to God's mission and helps us avoid turning it into *our* mission.

Okay, maybe this is something of a checklist, but notice that beyond the first conversation, you are on your own to the extent that God will guide the process from that point on.

In all of this, remember that you are *one* member of the body of Christ made of *many*. You cannot do this alone, nor should you. You need others. You may find yourself being asked to lead the efforts. That may be okay for a short time, but you must have an exit strategy. Otherwise you become the dentist trying to pull your own teeth.

The exit strategy will detail the work that needs to be done to empower someone else to take the lead. It doesn't have to be anything elaborate—just a plan that everyone is working toward fulfilling.

By doing whatever is needed to get things started we do our part to help "check, push, and adjust" the margins of expectations within our faith communities.

As advocates, we can work toward making certain accommodations standard instead of exceptional.

Chapter 7
Champions and Broken Hearts

In fall 2014 I attended the Catalyst Leaders conference in Atlanta, Georgia. Andy Stanley opened the two-day marathon of amazing teaching with thirty-four minutes of one of the most powerful messages I have ever heard, which has had a lasting impact on my life. I even have a copy of the message and watch it often, especially when I need a bit of encouragement.

He began by reading the first chapter of the book of Nehemiah and then asked us two questions:

"Who are you?"

"What breaks your heart?"

I was able to answer those questions immediately. What breaks my heart is that there are families like mine all over this country that cannot worship on Sunday morning because of attitudes about disability.

Then he asked another question. "What if your broken heart is part of a divine design?" And the kicker, "You have no idea what hangs in the balance of your decision to embrace the burden God has put in your heart." I was close to crying by the time he was done. I cry each time I listen to it even now.

I'd like to think I do have an idea of what hangs in the balance of my choice to or not to do something with my broken heart. Whenever possible, I set up an information table and talk to anyone who will listen about this great big portion of our society who have been not only neglected, but actually denied a faith community because of their challenges. Little did I know back then how many people were working on this already, and it is exciting when we share success stories. But there is still much to do.

Blessed with a Vision

My path was actually given to me many years before attending the Catalyst conference. When we lived in Maine, Matthias was assigned to a child development center that was thirty minutes away from home. There was no public transportation for that program, and thankfully the schedules allowed me to put Joshua on the bus for school and then immediately get on the road. Matthias was almost four years old. It had been that many years since we received the first diagnosis and two years living with the knowledge that both children had significant challenges. The first diagnosis was enough to tuck all our expectations of the future into a box and put it high on a shelf. The second diagnosis felt as if that box was encased in concrete and dropped off a bridge. I was at a complete loss about the future. As a newlywed couple, we thought we would both be involved in full-time Christian ministry. We wanted to be a modern day Priscilla and Aquila, Paul's friends who were an effective ministry team. But the dual diagnosis, so I thought, dictated there was absolutely no way that was going to happen. These two children needed constant supervision. They may be dependent on us for their entire lives. I had been around church my whole life, and even served on staff. I knew for certain those things were not compatible. We obviously had misunderstood that calling on our life.

A thirty-minute drive each way provides a person time to think. For me that time was usually consumed with mentally mapping out schedules or dreaming of the next craft project. One morning on my way home after dropping Matthias at school, I was listening to the Christian radio station, K-Love. The song "Go Light Your World" by Chris Rice started to play.

> *There is a candle in every soul*
> *Some brightly burning, some dark and cold*
> *There is a Spirit who brings a fire*
> *Ignites a candle and makes His home*

And as the chorus started to play, I am certain I heard the audible voice of God saying through the lyrics, "You still have a job to do. Go light your world."

Carry your candle, run to the darkness
Seek out the hopeless, confused and torn
Hold out your candle for all to see it
Take your candle, and go light your world

I was so overcome with emotion that I had to pull off to the side of the road to compose myself. In my lifetime thus far that is only the second time I felt like I was spoken to directly by my heavenly Father and absolutely the first time hearing Him audibly.

Those words challenged me to step back and look at our future with a bigger and much wider lens. Until then I had such a narrow view of what serving in full-time ministry looked like, I was completely missing the opportunity I had directly been given. My world was dark and lonely. I did not know any other caregivers but I knew they existed. We were all hiding in our dark and lonely caves of chaos.

I began to see in a more meaningful way what this passage of Scripture means:

> *Blessed be the God and Father of our Lord Jesus Christ, the Father of mercies and God of all comfort, who comforts us in all our affliction, so that we may be able to comfort those who are in any affliction, with the comfort with which we ourselves are comforted by God. (2 Corinthians 1:3–4)*

It now made perfect sense that I would experience all the things I had for the express purpose of being able to relate to and help others. Besides connecting with families, I also received a big vision of a place for families like mine to vacation. The concept of a respite, retreat and conference center was born, right there by the side of the road.

After composing myself and getting back on the road, I began to verbally work through what I had just experienced. "What we need is a place where families dealing with disabilities can go for vacation; even those whose kids tend to wander or have wheelchairs or sensitive medical equipment. What if this place took extra measures for those kinds of issues? It could have double layers of super high fence around the swimming pool, and sensors on doors and windows controlled by the guests. Every space would be wheelchair accessible. What about lifts in the bathrooms? We could really create a place where even the rare safety and accessibility concerns have been thought of and addressed.

"It would have cabins able to accommodate families and groups of any size. We need a small hotel-like spot with large sitting rooms. It needs to have sabbatical spaces, maybe with a huge garden, where clergy can come to relax or for small groups to come for planning sessions.

"A handful of small cabins would be reserved for families coming off the mission field and available to them as they transition to their next home. Other faith-based retreat centers are closing their doors because they don't have enough diversification of income. If we have a small working farm on the property, and maybe an 'old world arts' center that would provide studio space for artists and offer classes on a regular basis, we shouldn't have that problem. And maybe if it is located back home in the 'historic triangle' of Hampton Roads, Virginia, we can plug right in to that marketing vein."

"And it definitely needs a large multipurpose hall and a large commercial kitchen. Partitions would allow the space to be a multi-purpose room. Then we can truly market ourselves as an all-inclusive retreat and conference center option."

"This property needs to be big enough, though, to also have an assisted living facility for adults with autism or other non-medically fragile disabilities. There would be so many things they could choose to do as work on the property if they wanted. And best of all it would be an optional place for the boys after we were gone. And we need to call it Candle's Flame Conference and Retreat Center."

After talking to myself the whole way home and working through all that, I called my husband, who was fortunately on land and tried to tell him all about it. I had to give up because the words just weren't flowing intelligently, and he didn't really like talking about big stuff on the phone anyway. In my mind's eye I could see the whole map with trails connecting key spaces, strategically placed shade trees, bench swings, and bird feeders.

The business plan was in my head for years. Finally I drew it all out on paper. I know it will happen someday. This vision was and is an amazing gift.

The song says, "Go light your world." My world is among the disabled community. I had kept myself from participating in that world because the first glimpses were so unhappy. Support groups sponsored by the schools may have been important tools for others, but for me, seemed to encourage personal pity parties where few seemed to be able to pull themselves out of the mud their grief was creating. I didn't need any more of that. I was fully capable of creating and wallowing in that mud all by myself. And besides, that's not how God wanted me to live. I knew that and yet somehow found myself trapped during those first years.

On that day of my vision, I understood I still had a job to do. I needed to bring God's guiding light to moms and dads and caregivers like me.

Be a Champion

Are you willing to be a champion for faith and families in the midst of disability? Would you be willing to help check, push, and adjust the margins we function within? Perhaps this is super personal because you have a little one that needs extra supports. Perhaps you are a grandparent and completely at a loss for how to help that grandchild. If you are a mom or a dad in the midst of the challenges, I know you are exhausted. If you are caring for a parent or adult with a disability, you may be hitting walls you never knew existed as you simply try to live your life! The one in your care needs you to advocate for them. Or maybe they need to be encouraged to advocate for themselves? Grab hold of the freedom, and calling, we have to be advocates of change.

We all need the Body of Christ to acknowledge the worth and dignity of every human being. When we do that, all the rest will fall into place. I hope, after spending time in prayer, you will take a step toward being the champion the world around you needs.

Checking the Margins

Throughout this book we have looked at the margins we have forced ourselves to live within. Those margins are not inherently bad. Each of us must make that determination for ourselves. Your state of normal is yours and yours alone, and we need to guard ourselves against the judgement of others. How do our margins compare to the standard of love and acceptance given to us by God?

 ## Pushing the Margins

Are any of those margins too restricting? If we educate ourselves and others can we move those margins? If we spend some time in prayer, can we find the God given strength to do the necessary work?

Adjusting the Margins

God will honor this work as long as He is glorified in this process. Unfortunately, margins of grace are real even though there should not be a cap or limit to the favor or goodwill we extend to others. Jesus had no such limits. The body of Christ will gradually become more complete as we adjust those margins to recognize every person, child and adult, with a disability is indispensable. In so doing we might avoid being so surprised when the multitudes are gathered from every nation, tribe, people and language and stand before the throne of God one day.

> *After this I looked, and behold, a great multitude that no one could number, from every nation, from all tribes and peoples and languages, standing before the throne and before the Lamb, clothed in white robes, with palm branches in their hands, and crying out with a loud voice, "Salvation belongs to our God who sits on the throne, and to the Lamb! (Revelation 7:9–10)*

Chapter 8
Extras

If you have further interest in some of the topics addressed, I've included more information and suggestions here on theology, Vacation Bible School and accommodation ideas.

A Theological Perspective

What do you believe? How do you interpret the Bible? What are we supposed to glean from the Scripture that will have a profound impact on our life? For those who attend Bible colleges or seminaries, the study of theology helps magnify ideas and settle the answers to questions like these. That understanding then contributes to an individual's worldview.

George Barna has a great parent's study called *Revolutionary Parenting*. In that study an important piece is identifying our own way of thinking about specific subjects as an individual and also as a couple *before* it becomes an issue. This helps avoid arguments in front of children because a couple is in agreement and a child can't play one parent against the other. For example: What is our opinion concerning a daughter's wearing make–up? Or what time is bedtime? Or will we allow participation in the travel league that will certainly mean missing church?

These are all questions that require an answer and until they are discussed, they are a potential hotbed of contention under the right circumstances. So if we discuss the question *before* the young one is standing in front of us with big brown eyes and cute smiles, you will be able to be confident in your answer, and your integrity rises.

My children did not, and still do not, communicate like most. They are non–verbal. When we realized neither may be able to communicate well enough to understand the grace of God, I was really distressed. Our faith is so much a part of our lives, and we took our mission as parents to teach our children very seriously. As Scripture says,

> *You shall teach them diligently to your children, and shall talk of them when you sit in your house, and when you walk by the way, and when you lie down, and when you rise. (Deuteronomy 6:7)*

Teaching like this requires language. When we talk they are supposed to listen and respond with understanding or confusion, whichever the case may be. So what do you do when none of that works? I was overtaken by tears many evenings, dwelling on the idea that my children would not have a place in eternity with Christ because of their disability. Plenty of clergy told me not to worry about my children, but no one could show me in Scripture how that was true. Their denomination teaches that a person must make a verbal profession of Christ as Savior. How was my child, who couldn't do that, immune from the rules? As I described, I discovered the grace of God that covers them in their situation.

What follows is our family's Reformed Theological perspective. Your faith tradition may interpret these things differently, and that's okay.

Justified. The first scripture that quieted my anxiety over this was 1 Corinthians 7:14, which talks about the children of believing parents being holy. While it didn't feel like much, it was enough to prevent a complete nervous breakdown over the subject.

A bit later I would be reminded of Psalm 139:14 that talks about being fearfully and wonderful made in the eyes of God. Yes, the world sees a disability, but God sees goodness.

And later still we would agree that it is God's prerogative to save whom He will and we hoped the boys would be included. Acknowledging God's sovereignty is never a bad idea, especially when we feel we have zero control over a situation.

The Covenant Family. A long time after those initial discussions of our boys' salvation, I started doing research on the sacraments. The purpose was to suggest that our family members, and really anyone who attends church and has a disability, should be allowed to participate in covenant baptism and the Lord's Supper, even if they have not or cannot express an understanding the way everyone else does. That research was touched off by experiencing the Lord's Supper with my sons and hearing God specifically tell me my son was welcome at His table.

What I found would place all of my talking points in the context of covenant relationship. From the beginning, the covenant relationship included the whole family, even household servants. Every male in Abraham's household was circumcised to show belonging. When Christ came He gave us a new covenant. The new sign of belonging was baptism. Acts 15:1–35 solidified that clearly and definitely. Do you know how many households were baptized in the New Testament? How many times do we read in Scripture the blessings of salvation being extended to a single person—and their household?

How did we move so far from a covenant understanding of these things? Preliminary research suggests it's a long story. The major point to consider is that my children, because of the faith of their parents, are fully members of this New Testament covenant family. If we had been part of a faith community that baptized infants we would have done so. It is not a superstitious notion of salvation. It is an outward sign of belonging to the family of God.

The pastor of our church would baptize the boys at age fifteen and seventeen because of our new understanding of this covenant sign. They were baptized because we were being obedient to the guidance of Scripture concerning our children and signs of the covenant relationship. The boys did not object. In fact, I would certainly say they handled it with joy.

Our boys also participate in communion. They have never had a problem following our lead, waiting until everyone has been served. It is an amazing opportunity to talk about Christ's sacrifice because He loved us so much with the physical elements of bread and juice. Again, they have never communicated an understanding with words of what is happening, but sit quietly and reverently through the whole thing. Are words really that necessary? After all, it is the Lord's Supper, not mine. The table ultimately belongs to our Savior and King. Scripture such as 1 Samuel 9 and Luke

14 reinforce the idea that my boys are welcome at His table.

Sovereignty. When we truly embrace the concept of a God who is sovereign, many issues go away. I eventually stopped wondering if their challenges were all my fault because I ate too much tuna[28] or if it was vaccines.[29] I reached a point where I was no longer concerned about why my children were autistic and decided that is just how God made them.

My children were autistic because God needed them to be. He needed me and their father to see all the work that needed to be done in the church for the disabled. All this was planned since the foundation of creation! My children were autistic for God's glory, just like the blind man in John 9.

Romans 8 tells us that in all things God works for the good of those who love him and are called to his purpose. Romans 9 tells us that God will have mercy on whomever He chooses. I will trust that my boys have favor with God simply because He loves them.

---

[28] An article from 2004 suggested tuna can cause autism. As someone who had gestational diabetes, I ate a lot of tuna. https://www.telegraph.co.uk/news/worldnews/northamerica/usa/145444 26/Autism-linked-to-eating-oily-fish.html

[29] A simple search of "vaccines and autism" will yield a wealth of information on the controversy. In the early 2000's though, the debate was heated and so many concerned parents fell for the alarms.

Engaging Vacation Bible School

Some of our children learn best when we help them break down the steps of a task into the most basic parts. We need to do the same for this conversation. We must identify the small steps that we can celebrate as success and movement toward the greater goal. We cannot go into new situations with people we have no relationship with and expect anyone will listen to us as we tell them what they are going to do for us. When we ask others to do new or uncomfortable things on our terms, we aren't doing anyone any favors. Too many parents go into a situation and essentially say, "You will do this, and this, and this, and if you don't, you obviously don't care about my family and aren't real Christians." Few things frustrate me more than hearing stories of difficult parents unwilling to allow time for people to warm up and work through new requests.

You and your key advocacy partners need to know the ultimate goal, but you also need to identify the small bite-size goals that will slowly but assuredly get everyone to the desired destination. For example, let's say the big goal is that a child will be able to attend Vacation Bible School next summer. No matter the child's challenges, there are some basic steps to take to make that happen. Steps such as:

◊ Meet with the VBS director early – super early – At least six months in advance. Don't wait until the week before to tell someone you are coming, especially if they have no idea of your child's specific needs. *During this meeting you will reassure the director that you want to help make this VBS a success for everyone.* Be prepared to discuss what your child's strengths are but also weaknesses. Are there tough behaviors of which workers need to be aware? How do you mitigate those behaviors?

◊ Help create a training experience for all the volunteers that will help the crew welcome a wide variety of children with disabilities. (An "All Needs Crash Course" outline is available on the next page and also on the resources page at www.marginsofgrace.com/resources)

◊ Commit to help create or acquire class aids that will support all the children to be successful that week. Class aids such as picture schedules, fidgets for busy hands, cushions of air to sit on, and weighted lap pads can do wonders for helping kids of all abilities focus.

◊ Be present during the week of VBS, but don't assume you need to shadow or even teach your child's class. The whole point of training others is to equip them to be comfortable with whoever comes through the door.

Remember your goals. A personal goal in this example is for the child to be able to attend VBS. The organizational goal is for volunteers to be equipped and comfortable with working with children of all abilities. All these efforts should then be able to extend beyond VBS into the regular schedule.

Quick Accommodation Ideas for the Church

All the things we learn to support our loved one in the school or medical care environment can be applied to the church. For those with limited verbal skills, a system of picture exchange either with little laminate images on a Velcro board or within an electronic device is the method prescribed by most speech therapists. Those same pictures are often used to create a schedule of the day so everyone knows how the day is going to move along. It has been proven to reduce anxiety, which in turn decreases unhealthy or disruptive behavior.

Imagine if our children in childcare during the worship service had a schedule to consult that told them what they were going to do next while waiting for Mom and Dad to pick them up. The time would need to be purposefully scheduled to allow utilizing pictures, but it would address the needs of just about everyone. Pictures are so much quicker to process and if posted for everyone to see, they don't even require an adult to explain.

For those who can't handle loud places, what if the church bought a couple sets of noise canceling earphones to have available during large group time? Hang them close to the door and those who need them can be assured they may grab them and go. Even those without a diagnosis of some sort may enjoy more muffled tones.

Kids and the wiggles go together. It's tough for some kids to sit still for any great length of time. You can combat the squirmies with a few tools. Two of those tools are a textured cushion of air or a weighted lap pad. The textured cushion is inflated with a bicycle pump. It allows movement and sensory input that really does encourage them to stay seated. The weighted lap pad is also a wonder. They come in all shapes and forms. Some are just a heavy pad as big as a child's lap. Some have a pocket of gel with stars and moons or other fun bits that can be moved about. Remember, even if they are distracted by playing with one of these tools, chances are you are still being heard.

These are just a tiny sampling of options available to support differently-abled learners. Having these tools in the church setting communicates a level of "welcome" that cannot be achieved otherwise.

For More Information

There is a great deal of information out there today to help us with this subject. I am not going to try to list them all. Instead, visit this sampling of sites to find more amazing books and resources on the subject of disability and/or advocacy:

www.allbelong.org

www.faithinclusionnetwork.org

www.engagingdisability.org

www.joniandfriends.org

www.wrightslaw.com

www.marginsofgrace.com

Made in the USA
Middletown, DE
16 October 2022

12886990R00099